THE LAW
(IN PLAIN ENGLISH)®
FOR
ART AND CRAFT
Galleries

Leonard D. DuBoff

Interweave Press • Loveland, Colorado

Published by

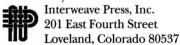 Interweave Press, Inc.
201 East Fourth Street
Loveland, Colorado 80537

Cover design by Susan Wasinger, Signorella Graphic Arts

ISBN 0-934026-87-4

Library of Congress Cataloging-in-Publication Data

DuBoff, Leonard D.
   The law (in plain English) for art and craft galleries / by
Leonard D. DuBoff. – 1st ed.
      p.   cm.
   ISBN 0-934026-87-4
    1. Art galleries, commercial–Law and legislation–United States.
  2. Art dealers–Legal status, laws, etc.–United States.
  3. Consignment sales–United States.   I. Title.
KF2043.A76D82   1993
349.73'024745–dc20
[347.30024745]   93-15983
                                       CIP

First printing: 5M:993:BC

▌TO THE MEMORY OF my mother-in-law, Cumi Crawford, for her love, and for the love and companionship of her daughter, Mary Ann, for more than a quarter of a century.

Foreword

▋ART APPEALS MOST TO THAT SIDE of our being that is most removed from the quotidian aspects of life. In art, we discover the delight of painting, the strength of sculpture, the intimate contact with the hands of artists in drawings and sketches. For many of us, art is a refuge from the pressures of our own lives.

So it is not to be wondered at that most of us who are drawn to making our lives and careers in the world of art do not think very much about its mundane, practical underpinnings. This is as true of the makers of art as it is of those who work in the marketplace for art. As a result, many are victims of pitfalls that could have been avoided through an awareness of how the law today affects all relationships, even—and indeed especially—those in the arts.

Fortunately, there now is a simple, straightforward guide for perplexed art professionals. In *The Law (in Plain English)® for Art and Craft Galleries,* Leonard Duboff addresses laymen in terms free of legal jargon. He sets up guideposts and, with great common sense and the benefit of long experience, outlines safe paths to follow. The book's store of advice is invaluable—and in this litigious age, essential for all who make their life and living in art.

André Emmerich
André Emmerich Gallery

Preface

▌THROUGHOUT MY PROFESSIONAL career as a practicing attorney and a law professor, I have realized the importance of pre-problem counseling. This is especially true in the field of art and crafts law, where many of the issues are complex and not usually understood by the attorney engaged in a general practice.

Creative people and gallery owners are often depicted as opposing teams in a tug-of-war. Nothing can be further from the truth. The individuals who create and those who sell their works are allies, engaged in a mutually beneficial relationship and making art and crafts available to the public. While there is a common interest shared by those who create and those who retail the creations, the legal issues encountered by each group are unique.

My goal is to sensitize art and crafts professionals to the law so that risky courses of conduct can be avoided, and problems can be spotted at an early enough stage so as to minimize their ultimate impact on the success of the business.

Although there are a number of books available for visual artists and craftspeople, there have been, until now, none for the art or craft gallery owner. This book is intended to fill that void and provide a readable source of information.

I have tried to present the most up-to-date analysis of the myriad legal issues that gallery owners and craft retailers encounter in their business activities. This book is not intended to serve as a substitute for an attorney; rather, it is designed to make you aware of the issues and options available in a host of common business situations and to provide you with sufficient knowledge to enable you to communicate effectively with a business attorney.

I sincerely hope that *The Law (In Plain English)® for Art and Craft Galleries* continues the tradition established by the other books in this series of providing an accurate, up-to-date, and readable text for an important segment of thc business community.

Leonard D. DuBoff

Acknowledgements

▮ THE IDEA OF WRITING A BOOK for art and craft gallery owners has been with me for some time. While I encounter many of the problems discussed in these pages during the course of my legal practice, the task of assembling this material into a readable text has been significant. Fortunately, I've had a number of friends, colleagues, and associates who have aided me with this project. It will be impossible to name and thank them all, even though they certainly deserve it, yet there are some to whom I would like to give special recognition.

I thank my research assistants, Michael Cragun, JD, Lewis and Clark, 1993, Christy King, JD, Lewis and Clark, 1993, and Troy S. Bundy, JD, Lewis and Clark, 1994, for their exceptional work on this book. I also thank Ormond H. Ormsby, for his help with the chapters on insurance and employee benefits, and Joe Markunas, CPA, and Ron Golden, CPA, for their help with the chapter on tax. My former legal assistant, Lynn Della, has been extraordinarily helpful with all aspects of this book, devoting countless hours to this project.

Stephen Kanter, Dean of Lewis and Clark Law School, has been particularly supportive of my research and writing in this field. Lenair Mulford of the Lewis and Clark Law School staff has once again devoted her exceptional skill to the Herculean task of converting a bunch of notes, scraps of paper, interlineated manuscript pages, and shards of all kind into a publishable book. Her skill and perseverance are truly praiseworthy.

My friends Hortense Green, coordinator of the Year of American Crafts for the American Crafts Council, Marilyn Stevens, editor of The Crafts Report, Laurie Rosen, editor of Niche Magazine, and Sunny Reedy, manager of the Images International of Hawaii Gallery chain, have been valuable information resources. Their knowledge and practical information have been very beneficial.

I am also extremely grateful to Linda Ligon, publisher of Interweave Press for her insight, intuition, and marvelous editing skills. Linda truly combines the soul of an artist with the skill, business acumen, and insight of a successful publisher.

My children, Colleen Rose DuBoff, Robert Courtney DuBoff, and Sabrina Ashley DuBoff, have also contributed to the quality of this book. They have each provided me with their unique level of help, support and, most of all, loving encouragement while I was working on this volume.

Last, but not least, I would like to once again acknowledge the indispensable contribution to this work by my wife of more than a quarter century, Mary Ann Crawford DuBoff. Her handiwork is evident throughout the pages of this volume, and it is her contribution that makes this work achieve the quality that it has. Not enough can be said to praise her input, support, and encouragement.

Contents

Introduction

▌ AFTER NEARLY TWENTY YEARS of on-the-job training in the gallery business, much of the material in Leonard DuBoff's latest book is familiar to me. How I wish this book had been available at the beginning of my career! *The Law (In Plain English)® for Art and Craft Galleries* is a survival manual for anyone entering or, for that matter, already in the commercial gallery world.

Mr. DuBoff's clear, straightforward approach makes a complicated subject easy to grasp. With explanations that are simple without being simplistic, he guides the reader through the essential stages of establishing a viable business. By demystifying many intimidating legal and business issues, Mr. DuBoff enables the prospective entrepreneur to focus more effectively on the creative and artistic aspects of this fascinating profession.

Often a gallery is founded by individuals with a strong vision, which, regrettably, is frequently undermined by a fuzzy business plan. A commercial gallery faces many challenges beyond that of making an artistic or philosophical statement. Clearly, the business must be an intelligently planned, efficiently managed enterprise if it is to survive. This goal is not easily met. With Mr. DuBoff's good counsel, however, the odds for success are in your favor.

Douglas Heller
President & Director
Heller Gallery

CHAPTER ONE
Organizing Your Business

■ EVERYONE IN BUSINESS knows that survival requires careful financial planning. Yet few people fully realize the importance of selecting the best form for the business. Every business has an organizational form best suited to it, and there are only a handful of basic forms to choose from: the sole proprietorship, the partnership, the corporation, a few hybrids, and the limited liability company, which is the newest business form.

Art galleries and craft retailers have little need for the sophisticated organizational structures utilized in industry, but because all entrepreneurs must pay taxes, obtain loans, and expose themselves to potential liability with every sale, it makes sense to structure one's business so as to minimize these concerns. When I counsel people on organizing their businesses, I usually adopt a two-step approach. First, we discuss various aspects of taxes and liability to determine which basic form is best. Once we have decided which form is appropriate, we discuss the organizational details, such as partnership agreements or corporate papers. These documents define the day-to-day operations of a business and, therefore, must be tailored to individual situations.

What I offer here is an explanation of the features, as well as some advantages and disadvantages, of the various organizational forms. I will also discuss potential problems but, because I cannot address the intricate details of your specific business, you should consult an attorney before deciding to adopt any particular structure. My purpose here is to enable you to better understand the choices available and to communicate more easily with your lawyer.

The Sole Proprietorship

The technical name *sole proprietorship* may be unfamiliar to you, but you actually may be operating under this form. A sole proprietorship is an unincorporated business owned by one person. Although not peculiar to the United States, it was, and still is, the backbone of the American dream to the extent that personal freedom follows economic freedom. As a form of business, it is elegant in its simplicity. All it requires is a little money and work. Legal requirements are few and simple. In most localities, you must obtain a business license from the city or county for a small fee. If you wish to operate the business under a name other than your own, the name must be registered with the state and, in some cases, with the county in which you are doing business. With these details taken care of, you're in business.

Disadvantages

There are many financial risks involved in operating your business as a sole proprietor, and the property you personally own is at stake. In other words, if, for any reason you owe more than the dollar value of your business, your creditors can force a sale of your personal property to satisfy the business debt.

You can buy insurance that will shift the burden of a potential loss from you to the insurance company, but for many types of business risks, insurance is simply not available—for instance, the potential risk that a promotional event, such as an opening, will be unsuccessful. The cost of liability insurance is also quite high and may be economically unavailable to some businesses. Even when procured, every insurance policy has a limited, strictly defined scope of coverage. These liability risks, as well as many other uncertain economic factors, can drive the sole proprietor into bankruptcy. If you recognize any of these dangers as a real threat, you probably should consider an alternative form of organization.

Taxes

The sole proprietor is taxed on all profits of the business and may deduct losses. Of course, the rate of taxation will change with increases in income. Fortunately, there are ways to ease this tax burden. For instance, you can establish an approved IRA or pension plan, deducting a specified amount of your net income for placement into the pension plan, into an interest-bearing account, or into approved government securities or mutual funds to be withdrawn later when you are in a lower tax bracket. There are severe restrictions, however, on withdrawal of this money prior to retirement age.

For further information on tax-planning devices, you should contact your local IRS office and ask for their list of free pamphlets. Or you might wish to consult an accountant experienced in business tax planning.

The Partnership

A partnership is defined by most state laws as an association of two or more persons formed to conduct, as co-owners, a business for profit. The economic advantages of doing business in a partnership form are the pooling of capital, collaboration of skills, easier access to credit enhanced by the collective credit rating, and a potentially more efficient allocation of labor and resources. A major disadvantage is that each partner is fully and personally liable for all the debts of the partnership, even if not personally involved in incurring those debts. Each partner is also liable for the negligence of another partner and for the partnership's employees when a negligent act occurs in the usual course of business.

In effect, each partner is considered an employee of the partnership. This means that if you are getting involved in a partnership, you should be especially cautious. First, because the involvement of a partner increases your potential liability, you should choose a responsible partner. Second, the partnership should be adequately insured to protect both the assets of the partnership and the personal assets of each partner.

No formalities are required to create a partnership. In fact, in some cases, people have been considered partners even though they never had any intention of forming a partnership. For example, if a friend lends you money to start your gallery, and you agree to pay your friend a certain percentage of the profits, in the eyes of the law you and your friend may be partners, even though that friend has no part in running your business.

If the partners do not have a formal agreement defining the terms of the partnership—such as control of the partnership or the distribution of profits—state law will determine the terms.

State laws are based on the fundamental characteristics of the typical partnership as it has existed throughout the ages and are, therefore, thought to correspond to the reasonable expectations of the partners. The most important of these legally presumed characteristics are the following:

1. No one can become a partner in a partnership without the unanimous consent of all partners.

2. All partners have an equal vote in the management of the partnership, regardless of the size of their interest in it.

3. All partners share equally in the profits and losses of the partnership no matter how much capital they have contributed.

4. A simple majority vote is required for decisions in the ordinary course of business, and a unan-

imous vote is required to change the fundamental character of the business.

5. A partnership is terminable at will by any partner; a partner can withdraw from the partnership at any time, and this withdrawal causes a dissolution of the partnership.

Most state laws contain a provision that allows the partners to make their own agreements regarding the management structure and division of profits that best suits the needs of the individual partners.

Taxes

A partnership does not possess any tax advantages over a sole proprietorship. Each partner pays tax on his or her share of the profits, whether distributed or retained, and each is entitled to the same proportion of the partnership deductions and credits. The partnership must prepare for the IRS an annual information return known as Schedule K-1, Form 1065, which details each partner's share of income, credits, and deductions, and against which the IRS can check the individual returns filed by the partners.

The Limited Partnership

The limited partnership is a hybrid form containing elements of both the partnership and the corporation. A limited partnership may be formed by parties who wish to invest in a gallery or shop and, in return, to share in its profits, but who seek to limit their risk to the amount of their investment. The law provides for such limited risk, but only so long as the limited partner plays no active role in the day-to-day management and operation of the business. In effect, the limited partner is very much like an investor who buys a few shares of stock in a corporation, but has no significant role in running the corporation. In order to establish a limited partnership, it is necessary to have one or more general partners who run the business and who have full personal liability, and one or more limited partners who play a passive role.

To form a limited partnership, you must file a document with the proper state office—usually the Secretary of State. If the document is not filed or is improperly filed, the limited partner could be treated as a general partner and, thus, lose the protection of limited liability. In addition, the limited partner must stay uninvolved in the day-to-day operation of the partnership. Otherwise, the limited partner might be found to be actively participating in the business, and thereby considered a general partner with unlimited personal liability.

Limited partnership is a convenient form for attracting investment when credit is hard to get or too expensive. Economic backers can share in the profits of an enterprise without undue exposure to personal liability. In return for investing, the limited partner may receive a designated share of the profits. From the entrepreneur's point of view, this may be an attractive way to fund a business, because the limited partner receives nothing if there are no profits; had the entrepreneur borrowed money from a creditor, he or she would be at risk to repay the loan regardless of the success or failure of the business.

Another use of the limited partnership is to facilitate reorganization of a general partnership after the death or retirement of a general partner. A partnership, remember, is terminated when any partner requests it. Although the original partnership is technically dissolved when one partner retires, it is common for the remaining partners to buy out the retiring partner's share— that is, to return that person's capital contribution and keep the business going. Raising enough cash to buy out the retiring partner, however, could jeopardize the business by forcing the remaining partners to liquidate certain partnership assets. A convenient way to avoid such a detrimental liquidation is for the retiree to step into a limited partner status. Thus, he or she can continue to share in the profits (which, to some extent, flow from that partner's past labor), while removing personal assets from the risk of partnership liabilities. In the meantime, the remaining partners are afforded the opportunity to restructure the partnership funding under more favorable conditions.

Unintended Partners

Whether yours is a straightforward partnership or a limited partnership, you want to avoid the unintended partnership. This situation can occur if you work with another person without formally describing your relationship in writing. If you do not, you could find that the other person is technically a partner and thus entitled to half of the income you receive, even though his or her contribution was minimal. For example, if you and another person decide to operate a retail craft gallery, you can avoid an unintended partnership by making that person a commissioned employee either by simply hiring the other person or paying him or her a percentage of what you are paid. Whatever arrangement you choose, put it in writing.

Cooperative Galleries and Shops

Historically, individual farmers who found themselves exploited by commercial buyers, or rural residents who could not purchase electricity from distant utilities, banded together to form cooperatives. Those groups were able to accomplish together what their individual members could not do on their own.

Forming cooperative galleries or shops is also an alternative for artists or artisans who have not yet found a gallery or shop willing to display and sell their works or who have chosen not to sell through traditional channels. The purpose of a cooperative is to pool the resources and talents of each member to benefit the whole group. Generally, each member works several hours to help run the gallery, and provides some items for display and sale. The members hold regular business meetings to make decisions about how the cooperative should be run.

The primary purpose of a co-op is to sell art and craft works. Members should be prepared (indeed hope) for at least one of their number to gain recognition. In such cases, the newly recognized artist or artisan may find it personally advantageous to leave the co-op and spend more time creating new work and pursuing more profitable commercial avenues for marketing his or her pieces. Remaining members will then be left to take up the departing artist's share of the work, dues, and other obligations.

There are many important factors to be considered when forming a cooperative. For example:

- Focus and goals
- How to resolve disputes
- How often the members will meet
- Fiscal responsibilities
- Procedures for admission of new members
- Size of the organization
- Staffing
- Type and frequency of exhibitions
- Promotional activities
- Commission structure
- Insurances
- Financial and other obligations of members, including contributions of money, time, and art work

Once these and other important issues have been decided upon, they should be embodied in a formal agreement signed by all members, and each member should receive a copy.

Artists are rarely trained in marketing and other business aspects of a gallery. It is, therefore, a good idea for the cooperative to hire or consult with an experienced gallery professional. Accountants, attorneys, insurance brokers and other professionals should also be consulted in order to ensure that the co-op complies with local, state, and federal laws regulating businesses.

A cooperative is essentially a kind of partnership, although it may be structured as any of the business forms discussed in this chapter for purposes of taxation, liability, and the like. Some have been set up as not-for-profit corporations; however, if the business generates a profit from successful activity and, if the members receive compensation, the organization will not be entitled to claim nonprofit status. It has even been held that a business engaging primarily in commercial activities, such as art or craft sales, whether or not it earns a profit, is not permitted to claim that it is a nonprofit organization.

For more information about co-ops, contact the National Cooperative and Business Association, 1401 New York Avenue, N.W., Ste. 1100, Washington, D.C. 20005.

The Corporation

The word corporation may bring to mind a large company with hundreds or thousands of employees. In fact, the majority of corporations in the United States are small or moderate-size companies. There are advantages and disadvantages to incorporating; if you find it advantageous to incorporate, it can be done with surprising ease and little expense. You will, however, need a lawyer's assistance to ensure compliance with state formalities, instruction on corporate mechanics, and advice on corporate taxation.

There are usually two reasons to incorporate: limiting personal liability and minimizing income tax liability. The second is particularly advantageous to a business that is earning a good deal of money. Corporations (and limited liability companies) are hypothetically legal individuals, and as such are responsible for their own acts and contracts. For example, if the gallery's kinetic art injures a collector, if the craft shop's car negligently injures a pedestrian, or if the glazed ceramic pot your store sold is responsible for lead poisoning, the corporation, not its owners, will be liable if the proper corporate formalities have not

been adhered to—such as holding proper meetings, keeping corporate bank accounts, and the like. Any individual personally responsible for a wrongful act will also be liable, however.

The Differences between Corporations and Partnerships

Like limited partners, the owners of the corporation—commonly known as shareholders or stockholders—are not personally liable for the corporation's debts; they stand to lose only their investment.

For the small corporation, however, limited liability may be something of an illusion because, very often, creditors will require that the owners either personally co-sign or guarantee any credit extended. In addition, individuals remain responsible for their own wrongful acts; thus, a shareholder who negligently causes an injury while engaged in corporate business has not only subjected the corporation to liability, but also remains personally liable. The corporate liability shield, however, does protect a shareholder from liability for breach of contract if the other contracting party has agreed to look only to the corporation for responsibility.

The corporate liability shield also offers protection in situations where an agent hired by the corporation has committed a wrongful act while working for the corporation. If, for example, a gallery employee negligently injures a pedestrian while driving somewhere on corporate business, the employee will be liable for the wrongful act and the corporation may be liable, but the shareholder who owns the corporation probably will not be personally liable.

Unlike partners, shareholders cannot decide to withdraw and demand a return of capital from the corporation; all they may do is sell their stock. A corporation, therefore, may have both legal and economic continuity, and in fact, it is common for perpetual existence to be established in the articles of incorporation. But the continuity also can be a tremendous disadvantage to shareholders or their heirs if they want to sell stock when there are no buyers for it. Agreements can

5

be made that guarantee return of capital to the estate of a shareholder who dies, or to a shareholder who decides to withdraw.

Whereas no one can become a partner without unanimous consent of the other partners, unless otherwise agreed, shareholders of a corporation can generally sell all their shares, or any number of them, to whomever they wish. If the owners of a small corporation do not want it to be open to outside ownership, transferability can be restricted.

Unlike a limited partner, a shareholder is allowed full participation in the control of the corporation through the shareholders' voting privileges: the higher the percentage of outstanding shares owned, the more significant the control. Shareholders are given a vote in proportion to their ownership in the corporation. Other kinds of stock can be created, with or without voting rights. A voting shareholder uses the vote to elect a board of directors and to create rules under which the board will operate.

The basic rules of the corporation are stated in the articles of incorporation, which are filed with the state. These serve as a sort of constitution and can be amended by shareholder vote. More detailed operational rules—called bylaws—should also be prepared. Shareholders and, in many states, directors have the power to create or amend bylaws. This varies from state to state and may be determined by the shareholders themselves. The board of directors then makes operational decisions for the corporation and might delegate day-to-day control to a president.

A shareholder, even one who owns all the stock, may not preempt a decision of the board of directors. If the board has exceeded the powers granted it by the articles or bylaws, any shareholder may sue for a court order remedying the situation. But, if the board is acting within its powers, the shareholders have no recourse except to formally remove the board or any board member. In a few more progressive states, a small corporation may entirely forego having a board of directors. In such cases, the corporation is authorized to allow the shareholders to vote on business decisions just as in a partnership.

Partnerships are quite restricted in the means available for raising capital. They can borrow money or, if all the partners agree, they can take on additional partners. A corporation, on the other hand, may issue more stock, and this stock can be of many different varieties: recallable at a set price, for example, or convertible into another kind of stock.

A means frequently used to attract a new investor is the issuance of preferred stock. The corporation agrees to pay the preferred shareholder some predetermined amount, known as a dividend preference, before it pays any dividends to other shareholders. It also means that, if the corporation should go bankrupt, the preferred shareholder will generally be paid out of the proceeds of liquidation before the other shareholders, known as "common shareholders," but only after the corporation's creditors are paid.

The authorization of new stock merely requires, in most cases, approval by a majority of the existing shareholders. In addition, corporations can borrow money on a short-term basis by issuing notes or, for a longer period, by using long-term debt instruments known as debentures or bonds. In fact, a corporation's ability to raise additional capital is limited only by its lawyer's creativity and the economics of the marketplace.

Precautions for Minority Shareholders

If you are involved in the formation of a corporation and will be a minority shareholder, you must realize that the majority shareholders will have ultimate and absolute control unless you take certain precautions from the start. Dissolving a corporation is not only painful because of certain tax penalties; it is almost always impossible without the consent of the majority of the shareholders. There are numerous horror stories of what some majority shareholders have done to minority shareholders. Avoiding problems is no more difficult than drafting an agreement among the shareholders. You should always retain your own attorney to represent you during the corporation's formation, rather than wait until it is too late.

Taxes

The last distinction between a partnership and a corporation discussed here is the manner in which a corporation is taxed. Under both state and federal laws, the profits of the corporation are taxed to the corporation before they are paid out as dividends. Because the dividends constitute income to the shareholders, however, the profits are taxed again as personal income. This double taxation constitutes the major disadvantage of incorporating.

There are several methods of avoiding double taxation. First, a corporation can plan its business so as not to show very much profit. This can be done by drawing off what would be profit in payments to shareholders for a variety of services. For example, a shareholder can be paid a salary, rent for property leased to the corporation, or interest on a loan made to the corporation. All of these are legal deductions from the corporate income.

The corporation can also get larger deductions for the various health and retirement benefits provided for its employees than can a sole proprietor or a partnership. For example, a corporation can deduct all its payments made for an employee health plan, while the employees pay no personal income tax on this benefit, whereas, sole proprietors or partnerships can deduct only a portion of these expenses.

The corporation can also reinvest its profits for reasonable business expansion. This undistributed money is not taxed as income to the shareholder, though the corporation must pay corporate tax on it. By contrast, the retained earnings of a partnership are taxed to the individual partners even though the money is not distributed. Corporate reinvestment has two advantages. First, the business can be built up with money that has been taxed only at the corporate level and on which no individual shareholder needs to pay any tax. Second, within reasonable limits, the corporation can delay the distribution of corporate earnings until a time of lower personal income of the shareholder and, thus, lower personal tax.

The S Corporation

Congress has created a hybrid organizational form that allows the owners of a small corporation to take advantage of many of the features offered by a corporate form, but to be taxed in a manner similar to a partnership and thereby avoid the double-taxation problem. In this form of organization, called an S corporation, income and losses flow directly to shareholders and the corporation pays no income tax.

This form can be particularly advantageous in the early years of a corporation, because the owners can deduct almost all of the corporate losses from their personal income, which they cannot do in a standard, or C, corporation. Also, they can have this favorable tax situation while simultaneously enjoying the shareholder's limited-liability status. If the corporation is likely to sustain major losses and shareholders have other sources of income against which they wish to write off those losses, the S corporation is probably the best form for the business.

Small corporation, as defined in the tax law, does not refer to the amount of business generated; rather, to the number of owners. In order for a corporation to qualify as an S corporation, it may not have more than 35 owners, who must be either human beings who are U.S. citizens or certain kinds of trusts. There cannot be more than one class of stock.

Taxes

S corporations are generally taxed in the same way as partnerships, although unfortunately, the tax rules for S corporations are not as simple as they are for partnerships. Generally speaking, however, the shareholder/owner of an S corporation can be taxed on his or her pro rata share of the distributable profits and may deduct his or her share of distributable losses.

Limited Liability Companies

There is a relatively new business form recognized in some states and being considered in many others. Limited liability companies, or LLCs, combine the limited liability features of a corporation with all of the tax advantages available to partnerships. Although the first LLC statute was enacted in Wyoming in 1977, it did not become an attractive business form until 1988 when the Internal Revenue Service issued a ruling classifying the LLC as a partnership for tax purposes.

An art gallery or craft retailer conducting business through an LLC can shield his or her personal assets from the risks of the business for all situations except the individual's wrongful acts. This liability shield is identical to the one offered by the corporate form. The owners of an LLC can also enjoy all of the tax features accorded partners in a partnership.

LLCs do not have the same restrictions imposed on S corporations regarding the number of owners, their citizenship, and whether or not they must be human beings. In fact, corporations, partnerships, and other business forms can own interests in LLCs. LLCs also may have more than one class of stock. There is, however, a restriction imposed on the transferability of the ownership interests in the LLC. Therefore, this business form may not be as desirable for big businesses as is the corporation or limited partnership.

Keep in mind that the LLC form is new, and so there is not yet any case law interpreting the meaning of the new statutes. Also, be sure that the state in which you will be doing business or in which you form an LLC recognizes the form. Only a handful of states now permit the creation of these business entities. Many states do not recognize the limited liability feature of LLCs, even if validly created in another jurisdiction, when they conduct business in those states. In fact, some states will not allow LLCs to do business within their borders.

CHAPTER TWO
Business Organization Checklist

■ AS DISCUSSED IN THE previous chapter, creating any of these types of businesses is a simple process, but to do it right and to make the most of all the advantages, I recommend you consult an experienced business lawyer. A lawyer's time, of course, is money, but you can save some of that money if you are well informed and properly prepared. Here is a checklist of some of the points you will need to discuss with your lawyer, which should help minimize the amount of attorney's time necessary to create your new business entity.

Other than you, the most important person with whom your attorney will work is your accountant. A Certified Public Accountant (CPA) can provide valuable input on the business's financial structure, funding, capitalization, allocation of ownership, etc. (See Chapter 22 for guidelines on selecting a lawyer and an accountant best suited to your needs.)

Business Name—Every business, regardless of its form, will have a name. Contact your attorney ahead of time with the proposed name of the business. In most states, a quick phone call or inquiry to the corporation division or Secretary of State will reveal whether the proposed name is available. Your attorney can reserve your chosen business name until you are ready to use it. You will also have to consider whether the business will have a special mark or logo that needs federal trademark protection or state registration. (See Chapter 13 for a discussion of trademarks.)

Checklist for a Partnership

If you have decided to conduct your business in the partnership form, it is essential that you have a formal written agreement prepared by a skilled business attorney to ensure the smooth organization, operation, and, when necessary, final dissolution of the partnership. You and your potential partners should devote considerable time and care to the details of your agreement before meeting with the attorney.

Some of the major considerations in preparing a partnership agreement include the name of the partnership, a description of the business, its requirements of capital and labor, the partners' contributions of capital and labor, duration of the partnership, distribution of profits, management responsibilities, duties of partners, prohibited acts, some features of future growth, and provisions for the dissolution of the partnership.

1. *Partnership Name*—Most partnerships simply use the surnames of the major partners. The choice then is simply the ordering of the names. Various factors may be considered in their arrangement—from prestige to euphony. If the partnership has a name other than the partners', that name will have to be filed with the state. Choose a name that is distinctive and not already in use. If the name is not distinctive, then others can copy it; if the name is already in use, you may be liable for trade name infringement.

2. *Description of the Business*—The partners should describe the basic scope of the business, its requirements of capital and labor and their contributions to those, and some features of its future growth.

3. *Partnership Capital*—After determining how much capital to contribute, the partners must decide when it must be contributed, how to value the property contributed, whether there is to be a right to contribute more or to withdraw any at a later date.

4. *Duration of the Partnership*—Sometimes partnerships are organized for a fixed duration or are automatically dissolved on certain conditions.

5. *Distribution of Profits*—There are any number of arrangements for distribution of profits. Although ordinarily a partner does not receive a salary, it is possible to give an active partner a guaranteed salary in addition to a share of the profits. Because the partnership's profits can only be determined at the close of a business year, usually no distribution of profits is made until that time. It is, however, possible to allow the partners a monthly draw of money against their final share of profits. In some cases, it may in fact be necessary to allow limited expense accounts for some partners.

   Not all of the profits of the partnership need to be distributed at year end. Some can be retained for expansion, which can be provided for in the partnership agreement.

   Whether the profits are distributed or not, each partner must pay tax on his designated share. The tax code refers directly to the partnership agreement to determine what that share constitutes, which further supports the need for a thorough and well written partnership agreement. If no agreement has been reached, the law presumes an equal share of profits.

6. *Management*—The division of power in a partnership can be made in many ways. All partners can be given an equal voice, or a few partners may be allowed to manage the business entirely, with the remaining partners given a vote only on predesignated areas of concern.

   Some consideration should be given to the unfortunate possibility of a dispute among the partners that leads to a deadlock vote and possible dissolution of the partnership. One way to avoid this is to distribute the voting power so as to make a deadlock impossible. In a two-man partnership, one partner might be in absolute control, for example (although this may not be acceptable to the other partner). If the power is divided evenly, however, between two partners or among a larger even number of partners, a neutral party or arbitrator should be designated in the agreement to settle the dispute.

   You should also specify who can sign checks, place orders, or sell partnership property. Under state partnership laws, any partner may do these things as long as they do so in the usual course of business. Such a broad delegation of authority may lead to confusion, however, so it's best to delegate this authority more narrowly. It is also a good idea to determine a regular date for partnership meetings.

7. *Prohibited Acts*—The list of acts prohibited to a partner can be an elaboration or expansion of the three fundamental duties that each partner owes the partnership by virtue of being its employee or agent. First is the duty of diligence. The partner must exercise reasonable care in his or her actions as a partner. Second is the duty of obedience. The partner must obey the rules that the partnership has promulgated, and most important, he must not exceed the authority that the partnership has vested in him. Finally, there is a duty of loyalty. A partner may not, without approval of the other partners, compete with the partnership in another business or seize upon a business opportunity that would be of value to the partnership without first disclosing the opportunity to the partnership and allowing the partnership to pursue it.

8. *Dissolution and Liquidation*—A partnership is automatically dissolved upon the death, withdrawal, or expulsion of a partner. This changes the legal relationship between the partners, but need not affect the ongoing business. The partners should provide in their partnership agreement for the continuation of the business after any partner dies or otherwise leaves the partnership, if this is the arrangement they agree to. Nonetheless, a partner who withdraws or is expelled, or the estate of the deceased partner, will be entitled to a return of the proportionate share of capital that the partner contributed. Exactly how this capital will be returned should be decided in advance, because it may be difficult or impossible to negotiate at the time of dissolution.

One method would be to provide for a return of capital in cash over a period of time. After a partner leaves, the partnership may need to be reorganized and recapitalized. Some provision should be made to define in what proportion the remaining partners may purchase the interest of the departed partner. Finally, because the partners may choose to liquidate the partnership, it should be decided in advance who will liquidate the assets, what assets will be distributed as such, and what property will be returned to its original contributor.

Checklist for Corporations and Limited Liability Companies

Decide first if the corporation will be an S corporation, where income and losses flow directly to shareholders and the corporation pays no income tax, or a standard C corporation, in which case it does pay income tax and corporate income is not taxed to the shareholders. Like S corporations, LLCs are not taxable entities, although the pass-through of profits and losses in an LLC is more analogous to the tax treatment accorded partnerships.

1. *Officers*—Decide who will be the officers of the corporation or LLC—that is, president, vice-president, secretary, and treasurer. State statutes generally require a corporation or LLC to have at least some chief operating officer, such as a president, or other administrative officers such as a secretary. It may be that the bylaws should have a separate description for specialized officers, but in very small corporations or LLCs, there probably will not be an elaborate division of responsibilities and titles.

2. *Shareholders and Owners*—How many stock shares should your corporation or LLC be authorized to issue? How many shares will be issued at the start of the corporation's or LLC's business, and how many will be held in reserve for future issuance? Should there be separate classes of corporate shareholders or LLC owners? For example, if you need to borrow money, you may want to issue preferred interest to the lender, rather than show the loan as a debt on the books.

If the corporation or LLC is family owned, ownership may be used to some extent as a means of estate planning. You might, therefore, also wish to ask your attorney about updating your will at the same time that you incorporate or create an LLC.

If your corporation has several shareholders, or your LLC has several owners, you'll want to find a way to prevent a voting deadlock. You may also wish to discuss with your lawyer possible precreation owner agreements that govern employment status of key individuals or commit owners to voting a certain way on specific issues.

3. *The Buy-Sell Agreement*— The first meeting with your lawyer is a good time to discuss buy-sell agreements. You'll need to specify what happens when one of the owners wishes to leave the business. Under what circumstances should he or she be able to sell to outsiders? In closely held corporations, the corporation or other shareholders are generally granted the

first option to buy the stock. Specify what circumstances—death, disability, retirement, termination, etc.—will trigger the corporation's or other shareholders' right to buy the stock. You might also want to tie the buy-sell agreement to key-person insurance, which would fund the purchase of ownership interest by the corporation or LLC in the event of a key owner's death. Also determine the mechanism for valuing stock or LLC interest, whether it be annual appraisal, book value, multiple earnings, arbitration, or some other method.

4. *Planning for Future Owners*—Are there plans to take on new investors or shareholders in the future? Do you intend to convert the corporation into one that is publicly held, that is, owned by a large number of investors? If so, the initial structure of the articles of incorporation and stock may be used as an important planning tool for the future. Although ownership interests in LLCs cannot be publicly traded, it is possible to bring in additional owners. You and your attorney should discuss how this might be accomplished in light of the legal restrictions imposed on the sale and transfer of LLC interests.

5. *Capitalization*—You and your attorney will work closely with your CPA to determine how best to plan this aspect of your business. You'll need to decide what the initial capitalization or funding of the corporation or LLC will be. Will the owners make loans to the business and contribute the rest in exchange for ownership interest? Owners may contribute money, past services, equipment, assets of an ongoing business, licensing agreements, or other things in exchange for ownership interest. What value will be placed on assets that are contributed to the corporation or LLC?

6. *The Board of Directors*—Decide who will be on the board of directors and how many initial directors there will be. It is a good idea for there to be an odd number in order to avoid a potential voting deadlock. Also determine whether owners will have the right to elect members of the board of directors based on their percentage of ownership, or perhaps by one vote per person regardless of percentage of ownership.

7. *Housekeeping*—Your attorney will need to know several other details: the number of employees the business anticipates in the next twelve-month period; the date the business's tax year ends; whether the accounting method will be on a cash or accrual basis; whether the business will authorize salaries for its officers; the date of the annual meeting of the board of directors and owners; and the name of the registered agent, if other than your attorney.

8. *Employee Benefits*—Be prepared to consider employee benefit plans such as life and health insurance, profit sharing, pension or other retirement plans, employee ownership programs, as well as other fringe benefits. If not implemented when the corporation or LCC is created, it is, nonetheless, a good idea to determine when or if such programs may be instituted.

CHAPTER THREE
The Business Plan

■ EVERY BUSINESS NEEDS CAPITAL at one time or another. This funding might come through bank loans or other conventional financing, through public sale of securities, or as venture-capital money. No matter what the source, the first step in obtaining capital is the creation of a business plan, which will enable the banker, venture capitalist or prospective owner to evaluate your company.

Creating a business plan also provides a useful opportunity for thinking about all the features of a successful business and to formally establish your goals.

The business-plan team—The development of a well-written business plan is a considerable undertaking. It forces you to focus your ideas, ferret out weak spots in your organization, and turn abstract concepts into concrete plans. Experienced professionals, such as lawyers and accountants, can provide invaluable assistance in putting together a sound and attractive business plan, and lend credibility to your numbers and projections. Your lawyer can help you obtain the legal protection your business needs while steering you away from the potential pitfalls that confront all new or expanding businesses. Your CPA can assist with the myriad financial assessments you must make.

In addition, experienced lawyers and accountants have invaluable contacts within the venture-capital and banking communities. They can tell you who has the capital, where it is being invested, and how you can best get a share. By enlisting the help of experienced professionals and following the suggestions presented here, you can develop a business plan that will help you attract the financing you need.

How to Structure Your Business Plan

The structure and content of your business plan will vary depending upon your company's stage of development, the nature of the business, and the type of markets it will serve. There are many different formats that have been used for business plans, although the order of presentation is, by no means, standard. The following topics should be addressed in every business plan.

Executive Summary

This section provides the reader with a short overview of the key elements of the business plan. Sophisticated business people are turned away by exaggeration, so the summary must provide an accurate appraisal of your business while distinguishing your product or service and organization from others that may be competing for the same funding. Include your key financial projections and the funding required to meet those projections. The summary should also describe your management team, and emphasize its experience and skills without ignoring its weaknesses and your strategy to overcome them.

Above all, the summary must catch the reader's attention. Unless the summary inspires one to read on, it has not served its purpose.

History

Business people want to know about a business's past performance before they assess its future potential. Toward this end, the business plan should provide a brief history of the business, including when it was founded; its subsequent development and growth; how it has been organized (as a partnership, corporation, LLC, or whatever); and how well past performance reflects future potential. If you have good reason to believe that the business's past performance is not indicative of future potential, be sure to state why.

Products and Services

This section describes in detail the products and services of your art gallery or craft shop. Explain any unique features and include a summary of present performance and status. Mention any special events and services, such as one-person shows and the publishing of prints, posters, newsletters, and catalogs. Keep in mind that investors are not likely to be art or craft experts but rather business people, so avoid jargon and be clear and specific.

The Market

This section describes the market your gallery or shop serves. If the work you are selling is particularly innovative, such as high-tech crafts, you may need to include independent market research to define both the initial and future markets. If the work you are selling is by recognized artists, the market has likely already been defined. In that case, you may rely on available data provided by the artists, similar businesses, industry professional associations, the National Endowment for the Arts (NEA), state arts commissions, etc.

For the purposes of obtaining investment capital, the market section may be the most important part of your business plan. To the banker, venture capitalist, or prospective owner, a business without a strong understanding of the targeted market is a bad risk, even if the work sold is first-rate. Consequently, the market description should be more detailed than the product description, indicating to potential investors that you understand the priority of market over product.

The Competition

Identify your competitors, discuss their relative strengths and weaknesses, and indicate the market share likely held by each. Include a forecast of the market share you expect to capture in the first three to five years, and the sources from which you expect to draw customers. Be sure to spell out your rationale for each projection—for example, more innovative art or creative crafts, marketing strategies, procurement of favorable reviews, competitive pricing, better service, or other factors. As with all projections in the business plan, be as accurate as possible. Do not understate the strengths of your competition while overstating your own. Sophisticated business people will not back a company that does not have a realistic view of its competition.

Source of Work

Obtaining sought-after art or craft work at an economical price and selling it expeditiously are the keys to profit making. In this section, describe the trade or other shows you attend; the artists or crafts people that comprise your list of clients and those with whom you have exclusivity agreements; the steps you have taken to expand your portfolio of work and the markets for it; and whether you acquire the work wholesale or on consignment. Also indicate whether you deal with resales or handle only newly created works. You should also present information about the reputation of the artists, including, for example, favorable reviews and relevant data from publications such as *Who's Who in America*, and the like.

Management

As a general rule, bankers, venture capitalists, and prospective owners prefer to invest in a start-up business with first-rate management rather than an established business with mediocre management.

Therefore, emphasize the experience of each key management executive. Include job descriptions and salaries, and provide resumes detailing your executives' past business experience, education, publications, and any other information that will indicate you have a qualified management team. If your management team has weak spots, define them and explain in detail how you intend to correct them.

Financial Data

Superior artwork and top flight management count for nothing if your financial projections do not show a substantial return on investment. This section is the bottom line of your business plan. Begin by summarizing previous financial performance. If your business is new, be sure that all projections are realistic and justifiable. Most prospective investors and lenders will check out other galleries or craft retail shops before making a financial commitment to your business. If your projections deviate widely from the industry norm, you will lose both the credibility and the financing you seek. Don't, however, inundate your reader with yards of computer-generated spread sheets. Your financial data should be concise and easy to understand.

Finally, your financial section should discuss the financing itself. Indicate how much money the business needs, the form of financing sought, and how the money is to be used. Most important, discuss the projected return within the next five years of operation. Again, be realistic and support your projections with solid data and a sound rationale.

CHAPTER FOUR
Borrowing from Banks

COMMERCIAL LOANS CAN BE a valuable source of capital. Lending policies vary dramatically from institution to institution, and although lenders by nature are conservative, some may be more flexible than others. You should talk to several banks to determine which would be most likely to lend to your business under the most favorable terms. To save time and increase the chances of loan approval, approach those banks first. (Your search shouldn't be limited to your community. You might have to conduct a statewide, regional, or even national search before you find the right combination of willing lender and beneficial terms.)

Once you've shopped the marketplace and selected a bank or banks, you're ready for the next step: preparing the loan proposal. It is very important to be properly prepared before taking this next critical step. Loan officers are not likely to be impressed by a hastily prepared application containing vague, incomplete information and unsubstantiated claims. Many loan requests are doomed at this early stage because ill-prepared applicants do not present themselves and their businesses adequately to the lender, even though the proposed ventures are, in fact, sound.

The Loan Proposal

To avoid an unexpected rejection, it's essential to know the bank's lending policy and follow its procedures for a loan application. At a minimum, you should be prepared to satisfactorily address each of the following questions when applying for a loan. The lender's decision will be based on your answers.

1. Is your business creditworthy?

2. For what purpose is the money needed? Do you need a short-term (one year or less) or long-term (more than one year) loan?

3. How much money do you really need?

4. What kind of collateral do you and your business have to secure the loan?

5. What are the lender's rules, and what limitations would apply to this loan?

Is Your Business Creditworthy?

The ability to obtain money when you need it may be as important to the operation of your business as having a good location and a rich portfolio of art or crafts. Before an institution will agree to lend you money, the loan officer must be satisfied that you and your business constitute a good risk—that is, that you are creditworthy. There are several criteria:

Do You Have a Good Reputation?

The lender will want to know what sort of person you are. Do you have a good reputation in the community and in your business? Are you known in the community? What is your past credit history, and what is the likelihood that you will repay the loan if your business falters or fails?

Despite its subjective nature, consideration of the borrower's character figures prominently in the lender's decision making. Often a loan officer will deny a loan request, regardless of how qualified the applicant appears on paper or how well collateralized, if not convinced of the borrower's good character. Even "signature loans"—which require only the applicant's signature and are available only to businesses and entrepreneurs with the highest credit standing, integrity, and management skills—have been denied on the basis of character.

For What Purpose is the Money Needed? Will the Loan be Short- or Long-Term?

Will you use the money to purchase inventory? To acquire fixed assets, such as display cases or light fixtures? Your answer will determine what type of loan—long-term or short-term—you should request. Loans for inventory purchases, especially if the business is seasonal (selling Christmas crafts, for example), will generally be short-term, and require repayment within one year or less. Short-term loans are also appropriate for facilitating the collection of outstanding accounts receivable. The bank anticipates that the borrower will be able to repay the loan quickly as the inventory is sold or the accounts are collected.

Intermediate-term loans, which require payment within one to five years, and long-term loans, payable within ten to fifteen years, are more appropriate for purchases of fixed assets (such as showcases, special lighting, computer systems). Repayment of these loans is not expected from the sale of the assets, but rather from the earnings generated by the company's ongoing use of them, which will occur at a slower rate. Hence the bank's willingness to allow repayment over a longer period.

Bear in mind that commercial lenders are interested in offering funds to successful businesses in need of additional capital to expand and increase profitability. They are not particularly inclined to make loans to businesses that need the money to pay off existing debts.

Depending upon your credit reputation, short-term loans may be available with or without col-

lateral. It is more likely that long-term loans will require adequate security, often necessitating a pledge of personal and business assets.

When and How Will the Loan be Repaid?

The questions of when and how the loan will be repaid are closely related to the answers to how much money is needed and for what purpose. You will have to convince the lender that your proposed use of the borrowed money will generate the additional revenue needed to pay the loan during the repayment period.

The banker will use judgment and professional experience to assess your business ability and the likelihood of your future success. The banker will also want to know whether or not the proposed use of the borrowed funds justifies the repayment schedule requested.

Once the bank has evaluated the creditworthiness of your business, you should be ready to explain the appropriateness of the kind of loan requested.

How Much Money Do You Really Need?

The lender will also be concerned that the amount of the loan be adequate, because an undercapitalized business is more likely to get into financial trouble. Similarly, a lender will be reluctant to approve a loan that is excessive, because the debt may create an unnecessarily high cash drain on the company. The loan should net the borrower the amount necessary to accomplish the desired goal, with a slight cushion for error, and no more. Estimating the amounts needed to finance building construction, conversion, or expansion (long-term loans) is relatively easy, as is estimating the cost of fixed-asset acquisition. On the other hand, working capital needs (short-term loans) are more difficult to assess and depend upon your type of business.

To plan your working capital requirements, it is important to know the cash flow of your business, present and anticipated. To help the bank in its evaluation, simply project all cash receipts and disbursements as they are likely to occur in each month.

Is the Cushion on the Loan Large Enough?

The lender will also want to know if you have included in the loan request a suitable allowance for unexpected business developments. That is, does the loan proposal realistically allow for the vicissitudes of operating a business and provide for alternative resources to meet your obligation if the business expectations are not met? Or is the borrower stretching to the limit, leaving no margin for error, so that repayment can be made only if the proposed venture is entirely successful? In the latter case, the lender may consider the loan too risky.

What Kind of Collateral Do You or Your Business Have?

Certain kinds of loans, called "signature loans," will be made solely on the borrower's signature. More frequently, banks will require collateral to secure the loan. Acceptable collateral can take a variety of forms. The type and amount of collateral necessary in a given situation will depend on the particular bank's lending policies and the borrower's financial state. In general, banks will accept the following types of collateral as security for a business loan:

Promises to pay by endorsers, comakers or guarantors—You may have to get other people to sign a note in order to bolster your credit. These people, known as sureties, may cosign your note as endorsers, comakers, or guarantors. The law makes some subtle distinctions as to when each of these sureties becomes liable for the borrower's debt, but in essence sureties are expected to pay back the borrowed funds if the borrower fails to do so. The bank may or may not require sureties to pledge their own assets as security for their promise to pay upon the borrower's default. This will depend, to a great extent, on the surety's own financial situation.

Assignment of leases—Assigning a lease as a form of security is particularly appropriate for a franchise. (For more information on franchises, see Chapter 6.) If the bank lends a franchise money for a building and takes back a mortgage, that mortgage may be secured by assigning to the lender the lease entered into between the franchisor and the franchisee that will occupy the building. If the franchisor fails to meet mortgage payments, the bank can directly receive the franchisee's lease payments to satisfy the franchisor's debt.

Security interests—Equipment loans may be secured by giving the bank a lien on the equipment you are buying. The amount lent will likely be less than the purchase price. How much less will depend on the present and future market value of the equipment and its rate of depreciation. You will be expected to adequately insure the equipment and to properly maintain it and protect it from damage.

Real estate holdings—You may be able to borrow against the equity in your personal real estate holdings as well as against those of the business. Again, you will likely be required to maintain the property in good condition and carry adequate insurance on the property for the benefit of the lender, at least up to the amount of the loan.

Accounts receivable—Many banks will lend money secured by your business's accounts receivable. In effect, the bank is relying on your customers to pay off your note obligation to the bank.

Saving accounts and life Insurance policies—Sometimes you may get a loan by assigning your savings account to the lender. Here, the lender will keep your passbook while notifying the bank that holds the savings account of the existence of the debt in order to ensure that the account will not be diminished during the term of the loan.

Loans can also be made up to the cash value of a life insurance policy, but you must be prepared to assign the policy over to the lender.

Stocks and bonds—Stocks and bonds may be accepted as collateral for a loan if they are readily marketable. Banks will likely lend no more than 75% of the market value of a high-grade security. If the value of the securities drops below the lender's required margin, the borrower may be asked to provide additional security for the loan.

Inventory—Business inventory, either on hand or to be acquired, can be used as security for short-term loans. This applies only to those works of art or craft that are owned and resold by the business, as distinguished from works consigned for resale. The lender will expect the loan to be repaid from the revenues generated by the sale of this inventory on a timely basis. Inventory may also be used as collateral for long-term loans when the lender establishes a so-called field warehousing arrangement. In this situation, the inventory is segregated and identified as collateral for a loan, and an employee, responsible to the lender, is placed in charge of the field warehouse.

What are the Lender's Rules and What Limitations Apply?

Once the loan has been approved in principal, the bank will likely impose certain rules and constraints on you and your business. These serve to protect the lender against unnecessary risk and against the possibility of your engaging in poor management practices. You, your attorney, and your business advisor should evaluate all of the terms and conditions of the loan in order to determine whether it is acceptable. If the bank's requirements are too onerous, it may be appropriate for you to decline this loan and seek alternative financing. Never agree to restrictions to which you cannot realistically adhere. If, on the other hand, the terms and conditions of the loan are acceptable, even though they are demanding, it may be appropriate to take the loan. In fact, some borrowers view these limitations as an opportunity for improving their own management techniques and business profitability.

When making long-term loans, the lender will be especially interested in the net earning power of the borrowing company, the capability of its management, the long-range prospects of the company, and the long-range prospects of the industry of which the company is a part.

The kinds of limitations imposed will, to a great extent, be the result of the bank's scrutiny of your company. If the company is a good risk, only minimum limitations need be set. A poor risk, of course, should expect greater limitations to be placed on it.

There are three common types of limitations you are likely to encounter:

Specific repayment terms—The bank will want to set a loan repayment schedule that accurately reflects your ability to earn revenues that will be sufficient to meet the proposed obligation. Risky businesses can expect shorter terms, while proven enterprises may receive longer periods within which to repay the loan.

Use of pledged security—Once a lender agrees to accept collateral to secure a loan, it will understandably be keenly interested in your assurance that, should the need arise, the collateral will still be available to satisfy the debt. To this end, the lender may take actual possession of the collateral if it is stocks, bonds, or other negotiable instruments.

Of course, a bank is not likely to take physical possession of a business's inventory or fixed assets and remove them to the vault. There are other ways by which a bank can obtain possession of your fixed assets while allowing you to use them. For example, the lender could perfect—that is, legally establish—a security interest in your fixed assets by filing a financing statement in the appropriate state or county office. (A security interest is the legal term for a lender's rights in collateral.) Real estate mortgages are perfected by being recorded in the appropriate government offices; security interests in inventory can be perfected for most purposes by either filing a financing statement or establishing a field warehousing system, or both. In these situations, the bank may impose restrictions on the use of the collateral and require that it be properly maintained and adequately insured. The bank may further limit or prohibit you from pledging the same collateral for any other business debts or loans.

Although this may sound reasonable, you should recognize that such restrictions could seriously hamper your ability to borrow additional funds if the need arises. For example, when inventory is used as collateral, you must find out exactly how much of your inventory is involved. A bank may ask for only a percentage of the total inventory to secure the loan. More likely, though, the bank's security interest will extend to all of the company's inventory on hand at any given time, including any inventory that is acquired later. Herein lies the potential problem: The inventory's value may well exceed the amount of the loan that it secures. Nonetheless, you may find yourself in the position of not being able to use any of the inventory as collateral for any additional loans. In cases where this situation is likely to arise, consider alternative sources of collateral.

Required periodic reporting—To protect itself, a lender may require you to supply it with certain financial statements on a regular basis, perhaps quarterly or even monthly. From these statements, the lender can see if, in fact, the business is performing up to the expectations projected in the loan application. This type of monitoring serves not only to reassure the lender that the loan will be repaid, but also to identify and help solve problems early on before they become insurmountable and threaten the business.

Analyzing Your Business Potential

The lender may inquire into any number of other areas related to your business, but if you are aware of the general information of interest to a lender, and can present this information clearly and articulately, you will greatly increase the chances of having the loan approved.

The lender will evaluate the business outlook for your company in particular, and for your type of business in general, in light of contemporary economic realities. Is it reasonable to expect that the proposed use of the loan will produce the anticipated increased revenues for your business? Your plan may appear viable on paper, but may not be realistic given the broader economic situation within which your gallery or shop operates.

Financial Evidence

Remember that bankers prefer to make loans to solvent, profitable, growing enterprises. They seek assurance that the loan will contribute to that growth, because your ability to repay the loan is directly related to your success. As I already mentioned, bankers are not interested in lending money so a business can pay off existing loans.

To help the bank ascertain the financial health of your business, you will probably be asked to provide two basic financial documents: a balance sheet and a profit-and-loss statement. The balance sheet is a tool to evaluate your business's solvency; the profit-and-loss statement summarizes the business's current performance. These financial reports are the principal means of measuring your company's stability and growth potential, so unless yours is a new venture, be prepared to submit reports for at least the past two or three years. Ideally, your CPA should prepare the documents so that they will be more credible in the event of an audit.

When interviewing loan applicants and studying financial records, the bank is especially interested in the business's recordkeeping methods, status of accounts receivable, type of inventory, and fixed assets. All of this information has a bearing on the bank's assessment of your potential success.

General Information

The lender will want to know whether or not the company books and financial records are up to date, accurate, and in good condition. Haphazard recordkeeping not only fails to reflect the business's true financial state, but demonstrates poor managerial skills. For obvious reasons, banks are reluctant to back sloppily run businesses.

The lender will also be interested in your accounts and notes payable. Are those obligations being paid on time? If you are not able to meet your existing debts, the lender will be hard-pressed to understand how you expect to be able to pay off a new loan. You may be seeking a loan to solve cash-flow problems you now have as well as to increase earnings and bring past-due accounts current while adequately handling the added debt. If this is your situation, you might overcome a lender's skepticism by presenting a solid, well-thought-out business plan that clearly demonstrates how the new loan will save, rather than add to, the business's financial problems and will boost revenues.

The lender will be interested in the size of your work force. Does it seem adequate to maximize the business's potential, or does it seem excessive compared to other similar galleries or shops? The lender will also likely want to know the salaries of the owner/manager and the other employees to determine whether or not they are reasonable. Excessive salaries drain a company's resources and profits, which may adversely affect the company's ability to meet debt obligations.

You should also be prepared to discuss your company's insurance coverage, the status of your tax payments, and if you sell work from samples or catalogs, whether there are order backlogs.

Accounts Receivable

A bank will be particularly interested in the number of customers that are behind in their payments to you, and how far behind they are. The lender will also want to know what percentage of the total accounts receivable are overdue. If any major account is behind in payments, the bank will want to determine the likelihood that this account eventually will be paid.

The status of accounts receivable is of special interest to a lender when the borrower is relying on those accounts to provide the cash flow needed to service the requested loan. You should also expect to be asked whether your business has an adequate cash reserve to cover questionable accounts, and whether the accounts receivable have already been pledged as collateral. A lender who secures a loan with collateral that has already been pledged to a prior lender will, in most cases, be limited in its ability to foreclose on that collateral if the debtor defaults. The prior lender has the first right to liquidate the collateral; subsequent lenders will receive only those proceeds remaining after the prior debt is fully satisfied.

Inventory

Because your business involves the sale of goods, the bank will need to know the state of the inventory on hand. Is it in good shape or will it have be marked down before it can be sold? Do you own the inventory or do you have it on consignment? Banks consider unpledged owned inventory as a possible source of collateral and also as a source of future revenues. The bank may also be interested in the inventory turnover rate, which reflects the demand for your business's art and crafts and helps to verify your revenue projections.

Fixed Assets

Because fixed assets can be used to secure a loan, the bank will likely be interested in the type, condition, age, and current market value of your company's fixtures, vehicles, etc. Generally, art galleries and craft retail stores have few fixed assets unless the business owns the building in which it is located. You should be prepared to explain how these assets have been depreciated, their useful life expectancy, and whether they have been previously mortgaged or pledged as collateral to another lender. In addition, be ready to discuss any need or plans to acquire additional fixed assets. On the one hand, this need could mean additional debt obligations in the near future; on the other, it could explain and justify your projected growth.

Options for Owners of New Businesses

A new business will not be able to supply as much information in its loan application as an established business will be able to provide. While this will not necessarily preclude the loan's approval, it could make it more difficult. You should, however, be aware that new business loans constitute only approximately 5% of all business loans made.

This reluctance to finance unproven businesses, which is understandably frustrating to new business owners, is consistent with the traditionally conservative nature of banks, which owe a fiduciary duty to their stockholders and depositors to disburse funds in a prudent, responsible manner. In light of the extraordinarily high failure rate of new businesses, compounded by the fact that a new business generally cannot provide adequate financial data to evaluate its potential for success, the lender is hard-pressed to justify making high-risk loans. Even when the new business borrower offers more than adequate collateral to secure the loan, the request may be denied.

Banks are comfortable lending money and earning profits from the interest charged on their loans. They are not comfortable in the role of an involuntary partner in the failing business of a delinquent debtor. Even though banks secure loans with a wide range of collateral, they understandably are not anxious to have to foreclose on that security. They are not in the business of selling art or crafts, or of trying to collect a delinquent debtor's accounts receivable. Although banks try to protect themselves by lending only a fraction of the collateral's market value, they still may not obtain the full amount that they are owed in a "distress sale" of that collateral, as this type of sale traditionally attracts bargain hunters who will often buy only at prices well below true market value. With an understanding of these dynamics, a potential borrower may better appreciate a bank's hesitation in approving a loan for a new business.

Banks do, however, make some loans to new businesses. You will need to demonstrate a good reputation for paying debts and offer evidence of business and management skills. Perhaps you have firsthand knowledge and expertise in the type of gallery or retail shop you propose to establish as a result of having been previously employed in the same or a closely related field. Emphasize that. In addition, provide a sound business plan to support your projections. You can further improve your chances of obtaining a loan if you have invested personal money in the business, indicating your confidence in its success. Furthermore, you should show, if possible, that the business has a good debt-equity ratio (that is, the amount of debt is low compared to amount of assets).

Even if your loan is refused initially, it is important to establish a good working relationship with a bank by keeping the banker apprised of ongoing progess and improvements. If the bank sees that your business is in fact succeeding, you will have opened the door for future financing should the need arise.

The Loan Application

Having analyzed your business in the terms you know are important to lenders, you are ready to develop the loan request. Although most lenders will require the application to include the same standard, essential information, they often differ as to the format. Some lenders may provide suggested formats; others may require a specific format. A simple application form and a conversation may be adequate for your local banker. The start-up business seeking substantial funds may be required to provide much more extensive documentation, including a detailed plan of the entire business. The actual content, length, and formality will depend on the lender's familiarity with your business, the amount of money requested, and the proposed use of the borrowed funds.

The business loan applicant is typically asked to

submit any or all of the following information.

1. *Personal financial statements.* These will indicate the applicant's personal net worth and will help the lender evaluate creditworthiness and repayment capability, as well as identify potential sources of collateral.

2. *The current year's tax return* and the previous two years' returns. Include returns for the individual and for the business.

3. *The business's financial statements.* As I mentioned previously, ideally you should submit statements covering the previous two or three years. They should be prepared and authenticated by an independent CPA. The lender may also request cash flow statements and profit projections.

4. *A business history.* This should include past profit or loss patterns, current debt-equity ratio, current and projected cash flow, and present and projected earnings.

5. *A business plan.* This plan should include an explanation of the proposed use of the requested funds and how the loan will benefit the business. The length and content of the plan will vary according to the financial health of the applicant's business and the amount and type of loan applied for (see Chapter 3). The lender may request other documentation depending on the circumstances—for example, if you are securing a loan against your house, the lender might request a title report.

The Loan Agreement

The loan agreement itself is a tailor-made document—a contract between the lender and borrower—that spells out in detail all the terms and conditions of the loan. The actual restrictions placed on the loan will be found in the agreement under a section entitled "Covenants." Negative covenants are things that you may not do without the lender's prior approval, such as incurring additional debt or pledging the loan's collateral or other business assets to another lender as collateral for a second loan. Positive covenants spell out those things that you must do, such as carry adequate insurance, provide specified financial reports, and repay the loan according to the terms of the loan agreement.

Note that, with the lender's prior consent, the terms and conditions contained in the loan agreement can be amended, adjusted, or even waived. Remember: You can negotiate the loan terms with the lender before signing. True, the bank is in the superior position, but legitimate lenders are happy to cooperate with qualified borrowers.

Communicate when problems arise—Once the loan is approved and disbursed, you'll have new obligations and liabilities. Of course, if all goes according to plan, the loan proceeds are invested, the business prospers, the loan is repaid on schedule, and all parties live happily ever after. However, the business world is fraught with uncertainty. If, for whatever reason, you are unable to meet the debt obligations, view the lender as a potential ally in solving the problem rather than as an adversary.

Bankers are not usually eager to exercise their right to foreclose on collateral securing a loan. In general, lenders prefer to work with a potentially defaulting debtor to help ease the burden so that the borrower can overcome the problems, stay in business, and reestablish the enterprise's profitability.

Lenders likely have no experience in marketing the types of collateral involved, nor do they want to run a distress sale which, at best, would probably bring in only a fraction of the money owed. Additionally, foreclosing against the business's assets further decreases the bank's chance of recovering any of the unpaid balance, because the borrower, stripped of the means to carry on business, is likely to be insolvent and facing bankruptcy. Even if the lender can liquidate the collateral at its current fair market value, that value may be well below the value agreed upon when the loan was made. For these and other reasons, banks foreclose on collateral only as a last resort.

Therefore, through experience, lenders have learned to identify a variety of red flags that indicate the debtor is experiencing financial difficulty. For example, the alarm sounds when loan payments are made later and later each month, or when the business's account shows increasingly more checks dishonored for insufficient funds.

When the lender sees these signals, the account may be assigned to a separate department set up within the bank to assist borrowers in a variety of ways: repayment terms can be extended, the amount of payment due each month can be temporarily reduced, or the bank may accept repayment of interest only, until the business has overcome its difficulties. The bank may also offer advice for solutions to the problem, particularly if poor management is the source of the difficulties.

To what extent the bank will be willing to accommodate a delinquent debtor very often depends on the debtor's attitude and cooperative spirit. At the first sign of trouble, the borrower should notify the bank that there is a problem, explain what is being done to remedy the situation, and keep the bank informed on a regular basis of the progress being made. It's unreasonable to expect a bank to be sympathetic and make concessions if you've waited until the debt is long past due before attempting to discuss the problem. A bank is also not likely to be too sympathetic toward a borrower who fails to return phone calls or is always "unavailable" to discuss the problem.

A solid professional relationship with your lender can be an invaluable asset to your business, not only for procuring loans but for help in difficult times. The ultimate success and growth of your business may well depend on it.

CHAPTER FIVE
On Getting Paid

■ IN AN IDEAL WORLD, EVERY ONE of your gallery or craft retail sales would be for cash at the time of sale. Unfortunately, we do not live in an ideal world, and a host of problems can and do arise when dealing with customers. Fortunately, there are several methods to deal with these problems, ranging from preventive action to initiating a lawsuit.

If you are fortunate enough to deal with people who always pay in cash on delivery, then this chapter may be of no concern to you. If you have experienced problems with or delays in payment, however, or have had some totally uncollectible bills, here are some useful suggestions.

Point-of-Sale Payments

When payment is made by currency, check, or credit card, the prudent art gallery owner or crafts retailer should determine whether the currency is authentic, whether the check is going to be paid by the bank, or whether the credit card will be honored.

Currency

Occasionally, it is simple to identify counterfeit currency—for example, if the counterfeiter has put George Washington on a $5 bill. Usually, however, the irregularities are much more subtle, and identification is very difficult. The best way to avoid being stuck with a counterfeit bill is to keep your eyes open. The federal government is quite diligent in alerting business people to the presence of counterfeit currency in a particular area when possible.

Credit Cards

To avoid credit card fraud, the first thing to do is to compare the signature on the back of the card with the signature on the transaction slip. Even more important is to follow the credit card company's procedures carefully. If the company requires you to get authorization for all credit card sales over $50, be sure to get that authorization. Although the procedure may seem time-consuming and troublesome, it is well worth the effort. If you have made a credit card sale without following the correct procedure, and the credit card has been stolen or is otherwise invalid, or the buyer has exceeded the credit limit, you are likely to be stuck with the loss.

Personal Checks

The most frequent difficulty occurs with payments made by personal checks. The person who writes the check may be an imposter with someone else's checkbook, for example. Even if the individual writing the check is legitimate, other situations can prevent the check from being honored by a bank. One of the most common difficulties is the problem of insufficient funds to cover the check. If the amount of your sale is substantial, you might be wise to request a certified, cashier's or bank-guaranteed check. This, however, may deter impulse purchases, and may not be practical for many art galleries and craft retailers.

If the person writing the check is known to the recipient, the risk of fraud is reduced, but if the sale is to a stranger, you should verify the purchaser's address and phone number with supporting pieces of identification, even if the information is printed on the check. Insist upon seeing at least two pieces of identification, one of which should have a photograph of the person who is writing the check. (Many states require photographs on drivers' licenses.) A current major credit card, or a check guarantee card with photo and signature facsimile are also good. Do not accept as identification such items as a Social Security card, a library card, or any identification that can easily be obtained or forged. Also be wary of an individual presenting a check from a bank well beyond the local area, vacationers notwithstanding.

Watch the person sign the check (presigned checks could have a traced signature), and compare that signature with the signatures on the two forms of identification. Only an expert can identify a good forgery, but you may be able to catch the clumsy attempts of amateurs.

To further protect yourself, accept checks only if they are made out to you and are written for the exact amount of the sale. Do not take checks made out to someone else and endorsed to you, and never cash a check.

Another way to minimize the possibility of obtaining a bad check is to subscribe to a check verification service, such as Telecheck or Check-Rite (consult your telephone directory for local branches). These businesses maintain computer logs of individuals and businesses whose checks written to other service subscribers have been dishonored. By simply making a telephone call or entering the customer's driver's license number or other identifiers into the service's data bank, you can discover if the customer has a history of negotiating bad checks.

Despite all these precautions, some bad checks do slip through. In most states it is a crime to obtain property with a bad check. If the person can be found, you can bring a lawsuit to recover the amount of the check. If you win the suit, most states will allow the recovery of damages and reasonable costs of litigation, including reasonable attorney's fees.

Installment Sales

Generally, when work is delivered to a customer, the seller has the legal right to demand payment in full at that moment. One exception to this rule, common to art and craft dealers, is the installment purchase, in which the buyer takes possession of the work before full payment is made.

If your gallery or shop permits installment sales, you can offer at least two types of arrangements: a "layaway plan," or sales on credit.

The layaway plan is the safest as it requires the purchaser to make full payment before the work is delivered. The purchaser signs a written agreement that sets forth the terms of the layaway plan, which include:

- The full purchase price to be paid

- The amount of down payment, if any

- The amount of each installment payment and the date it is due

- Provisions for nonperformance, such as nonpayment by the buyer after a certain date or destruction of the work while in the seller's possession

- Rate of interest charged on the credit purchase, if any

- Penalties for late payment

The sale on credit is less common. The purchaser obtains possession of the work before full payment is made. For this, too, you should have a written agreement signed by the purchaser covering the terms of the arrangement. The contract should include essentially the same terms as a layaway contract, except that it should reflect the fact that the purchaser has possession of the work. The contract should require the purchaser to insure the work for the benefit of the seller during the term of the contract, and should also include a provision permitting the seller to reclaim the work in the event of the buyer's default.

A dealer may legally protect its interest in the work by having the purchaser sign a Uniform Commercial Code Financing Statement (UCC-1) and filing it in the appropriate government office(s)—usually the Secretary of State. The Uniform Commercial Code (UCC) is a body of commercial law that provides rules of commercial practice and has been enacted in every state and territory of the United States except Louisiana (which has adopted a comparable code). Article 9 of the UCC provides a method whereby dealers can give public notice of their interest in a work lawfully in the possession of a buyer or other party and sets forth the procedure for foreclosing the security interest in the event of default. You should consult with your lawyer when establishing your credit sales program.

Rental Sales

Many art galleries and some craft retailers have established a rental sales program, which permits an individual to possess the work for a limited time before payment is due. This type of arrangement allows the individual to live with the work in order to decide whether or not to purchase it, or to use it solely as a temporary decoration. In both situations, the dealer has relinquished possession of the work to someone who has not paid for it and may never buy it. A written agreement is essential.

The contract should identify the work and should specify the term of the agreement; the amount of each rental payment and date it is due, including any initial payment; any late charges or other assessments; a provision for insurance of the work; purchase price of the work and terms if the rental is converted to a sale, including the applicability to the purchase price of any rental payments; location of the work during the rental period; and default provisions. In addition, the

dealer's interest in the work should be secured by use of a UCC-1 Financing Statement signed by the renter, and filed in the appropriate government office(s) by the dealer. (See the sample rental agreement on p. 117).

If Payment Never Comes

Common sense, diligence, and attention to detail are always important attributes for any business person. When the economy is weak and money is tight, they become essential. There will probably always be some deadbeats and some uncollectible bills, but with proper care and attention, you can keep these to a minimum. For the most part, careful screening of customers will minimize the need to collect payment for sales. In some instances, however, you may need to send follow-up bills or resort to legel remedies available to you, either directly or through a collection agency.

If you have extended store credit or if work is on a rental program and you have perfected your security interest in the work, then you may regain possession of the work or payment for it by complying with the rules set forth in Article 9 of the UCC for foreclosure. Work with an experienced business lawyer when pursuing your remedies under the Code.

If you have not perfected your security interest, there are essentially three other alternatives for you to obtain payment.

The first possibility is to do nothing. If the amount is small enough, you may simply decide not to pursue collection. Needless to say, you should then refrain from doing any future business with that customer. The amount you spent on the lost inventory should be deductible as a business loss.

Lawsuit

A second option is the instigation of a full-scale lawsuit to force payment. In many states, a formal demand for payment must be made prior to commencing a lawsuit. This option is practical only if the outstanding debt is relatively large. It is customary to hire an attorney, and this will likely be quite expensive, particularly if the case goes to trial.

The fees charged for filing a case may be $100 or more, depending on the jurisdiction, and must be paid when the case is started. The debtor must be served with notice of the suit, for which you often need to hire a process server—an expensive proposition. Most states permit alternative forms of service. For example, "constructive service" may be made by publication and/or mailing. Enlist the aid of an experienced litigation lawyer if you're contemplating this form of collection.

Even if the case is won, the buyer may still refuse to pay, and you'll have to initiate further proceedings to enforce payment—for example, the garnishing of wages, seizing of the debtor's property, or placing liens on houses or bank accounts. All in all, the expense involved in a civil trial may amount to more than the debt itself.

Small Claims Court

A simpler and less expensive option is to bring an action in small claims court. The name of this court and the rules may vary from state to state, but all of the systems are geared toward making the process as swift, accessible, and as inexpensive as possible. In many states, hearings on small claim actions may even be held on weekends or evenings, which is more convenient.

The major savings in a small claims court proceeding is due to the fact that attorneys are customarily not permitted in such courts, unless they represent themselves or a corporation. Even in states where attorneys are not specifically barred by statute, the court rules are set up in such a clear, comprehensible way that an attorney is usually not needed. Most small claims courts have staff members who will guide you through the pleading and practice.

The procedure in the hearing is quite simple. The judge simply hears both sides of the case and allows the testimony of any witnesses or evidence either party has to offer. Jury trials are never permitted in small claims court, although the defendant may be able to have the case moved to a con-

ventional court if he or she desires a trial by jury.

Not all actions, however, can be brought in small claims court. As the name implies, only claims for small amounts can be made. The definition of small ranges from a maximum of $100 in New Jersey's municipal court to a $6,000 maximum in Indiana's small claims court. Moreover, only suits for monetary damages are appropriate for small claims court; other forms of relief, such as an injunction or specific performance (which requires the terms of the contract to be performed), cannot be obtained there.

Once initiated, the small claims court process is relatively swift and inexpensive. Filing fees are generally around $50. In some courts, the creditor is not itself responsible for informing the debtor that suit has been brought. Instead, the clerk of the court will mail the notice to the defendant by certified or registered mail, and the creditor is charged a small fee to cover mailing costs. Other states require personal service, which is often handled by the sheriff's office for a fee.

An action in small claims court has some disadvantages. First, the judgment is often absolutely binding: neither party may appeal. Where appeal is allowed, as in New York state, the party wishing to challenge the judgment must show that "substantial justice has not been done." This is not easy.

The other major disadvantage of small claims action is that the judgment may be uncollectible. In many states, the usual methods of enforcing a judgment, such as the garnishment of wages or liens against property, are unavailable to the holder of a judgment from small claims court. In other states, New York, for example, enforcement action can be taken only if the debt is the result of a business transaction and the debtor has three other outstanding small claims court judgments.

Bankruptcy

Occasionally you may find that the person who owes you money has filed for protection under the bankruptcy laws. Or due to extensive collection or other financial problems, you may find that filing for bankruptcy is the appropriate solution for your business.

There are two general categories of business bankruptcy: straight bankruptcy and reorganization. Creditors customarily receive more of the debt due in the case of a reorganization than they do in the case of a straight bankruptcy. Reorganization is feasible, however, only when a healthy business is suffering from a temporary economic reversal.

Straight bankruptcy

Straight bankruptcy, also referred to as Chapter 7 of the Bankruptcy Code, provides for the prompt conversion of all of the bankrupt's nonexempt property or assets to cash, from which the creditors are paid. In an "asset" case, the creditor must file a claim within the time specified in the court's notice of filing, or the claim will be disallowed. In a "no-asset" case, however, the creditor may not file a claim and there will be no recovery.

The Bankruptcy Code gives certain categories of creditors priority for payment, such as the U.S. government for taxes, employees for wages owed, and secured parties for the amount of their security interests. Each category of creditor must be paid in full before the next category of creditor can be paid. If there is not sufficient money to satisfy all creditors in a particular category, the members of that group will receive a proportionate share.

In addition, not all of the bankrupt's assets are available for creditors—for example, a modest house, a holy book, clothing, and the like. The list of exempt property varies from state to state.

After the bankrupt's nonexempt assets are completely distributed, and the bankrupt has fulfilled all requirements of the Bankruptcy Code, the judge discharges—or wipes out—the bankrupt's debts. There are some claims, however, that cannot be discharged in bankruptcy. The claim of any creditor who was not notified of the bankruptcy and who therefore did not participate remains viable even after the proceeding has ended. Similarly, certain judgments, for wrongful acts and fraud, for example, also cannot be discharged.

Reorganization

The second type of bankruptcy proceeding, the so-called Chapter 11 or reorganization, entails a different process. Rather than terminating the business, a Chapter 11 is designed to facilitate an orderly payment to creditors so that the business may survive.

When the Chapter 11 petition is filed, the creditors and debtor meet and the debtor proposes a reorganization plan. Any legal proceedings for debt collection other than the bankruptcy proceeding are frozen, and the bankrupt is given the opportunity to satisfy its creditors. The creditors may participate in drafting the plan. If a plan acceptable to all creditors is prepared in a timely fashion, it is presented to the bankruptcy judge. If the judge determines it is "fair and equitable", the reorganization plan is implemented.

If the plan satisfies any of the three following criteria, it will be judged "fair and equitable" to the secured creditors. In order to have the plan accepted by all the creditors, a secured creditor may be forced to take a less favorable position than the UCC would allow. Even though that may happen on occasion, a gallery or crafts retailer with a security interest is still far better off than one who is unsecured.

- The secured creditors retain their liens and receive future cash payments equal to the value of the security

- The secured parties retain a lien on the proceeds from the sale of their collateral, or

- The secured creditors receive the equivalent of their interests, such as cash up front or substituted collateral

If a Chapter 11 reorganization plan, even once it has been confirmed, proves unfeasible, the bankruptcy may be converted by the bankrupt to a Chapter 7 proceeding.

CHAPTER SIX
Franchises

■ ONCE ESTABLISHED, A GALLERY owner or craft retailer may wish to expand its business in order to enlarge its market. Franchising can present this opportunity to those without the capital resources to branch out on their own. You may franchise an already successful operation by selling the rights and tools necessary to replicate the business in other locations. Galleries and craft retailers who are struggling with their independently owned businesses might find that buying into an existing franchise or augmenting inventory with a franchised product line will keep the doors open. Successful franchises offer a proven, well-run format and a good support network that is reassuring to both potential franchisees and customers.

A franchise should be distinguished from a chain. In a chain operation, one business owns all of the outlets, which are run as a single network. In a franchise, the franchisor provides the plan, education, ongoing support, market research, and perhaps even the products to a franchisee, who is an independent business operator.

Franchises generally fill a specific niche while providing the public with a marketable product or service. Many of these operations focus on customer service, because much revenue is generated by repeat customers. The concept has been successful in several types of businesses—such as McDonalds in the fast-food business and Midas in the auto-repair business. In the art and crafts field, several picture-framing businesses and stained-glass operations, for example, have successfully applied the concept of franchising.

Creating a Franchise

If you have decided to franchise your business, you'll need the following to ensure success:

- A well-established, profit-generating business, which may be used as a prototype. Franchisors should take care not to permit franchisees to be located too close to one another, so as not to compete with each other.

- Executives who understand the industry and consultants who understand the legal and business aspects of franchising. In order to ensure that you have top-quality franchisees, you may want to recruit from among your present employees who are already familiar with you and the products and philosophy of your company.

- Adequate capital to launch the program and provide initial and ongoing support for franchisees.

- A unique and protectable trademark that has been registered on both the state and federal levels (see Chapter 13 for more information on trademarks).

- Quality-control standards, particular to your type of business.

- A franchisee training program.

- A support staff network for franchisees, such as a newsletter, monthly meetings, or a computer link, again depending on your business.

- Thorough knowledge of the industry and understanding of the competition.

- Legal documents, prepared by experienced lawyers and accountants complying with Federal Trade Commission (FTC) and franchising law regulations.

States typically designate as franchise agreements those agreements that specify that (1) a franchisee is allowed to offer, sell, or distribute goods or services according to a plan developed by the franchisor; (2) the franchisee's business under the plan is identified by the franchisor's trademark, service mark, trade name, logo, etc.; and (3) the franchisee is required to pay the franchisor or give something of value for the right to conduct business under the plan.

About one third of the states require that franchise opportunities be registered before the actual sale. Additionally, all franchisors must file with federal regulatory agencies and prepare disclosure statements for publication in the FTC's Uniform Offering Circular. Among other things, the following must be presented in the disclosure statement:

1. The identity of the franchisor, its franchisees, and their track records.

2. A description of the business experience of the franchisor's officers, directors, and managers.

3. Particulars of any law suits in which the franchisor or its officers, directors, and managers have been involved.

4. Details of any previous bankruptcies declared by the franchisor, its officers, directors, and managers.

5. The initial franchise fee and any other initial costs required to obtain the franchise.

6. Payments required after the franchise has opened, which will vary according to the agreement.

7. Quality control restrictions, including authorized suppliers.

8. Assistance available to the franchisee from the franchisor.

9. Inventory restrictions, such as permission to sell only those materials supplied by the franchisor.

10. Territorial restrictions and protections.

11. Conditions required for franchise renewal or conditions under which renewal may be denied by the franchisor, the franchise may be transferred to a third party by the franchisee, or either party may terminate or modify the agreement.

12. Training programs available to the franchisee.

13. Any celebrities or public figures involved in the franchise.

14. Site-selection assistance offered to franchisee from franchisor.

15. Statistical information about the number of existing franchises and number of projected future franchises, as well as the number of franchises terminated, not renewed, and repurchased by the franchisor in the past.

16. The franchisor's financial statement.

17. The extent to which the franchisee is required to participate in the operation of the franchise.

18. The basis for any earnings promises made to the franchisee, including the percentage of existing franchises that have achieved the results promised.

19. The names and addresses of other franchisees.

Purchasing a Franchise

If you are interested in purchasing a franchise, check closely to see that the franchisor has complied with all of the steps outlined above. Additionally, make sure the opportunities and returns you desire are actually being offered.

Whether buying or selling, always have franchise plans double-checked by competent accounting and legal professionals.

For those craft retailers and gallery owners looking to augment their inventory with franchised products or to convert faltering ventures into franchises, a good resource is the Franchise Opportunity Handbook, published by the U.S. Department of Commerce. This book lists most registered franchise opportunities, with a brief description of the business, the franchise fee, and the relationship between franchisor and franchisee.

Additional information about franchises, including books, publications, tapes, and video cassettes, is available from the International Franchise Association, 1350 New York Avenue N.W., Suite 900, Washington, D.C. 20005. The International Franchise Association sponsors World of Franchising Expos across the country. For more information, write to: IFA Expos, c/o The Blenheim Group, 1133 Louisiana Avenue, Suite 210, Winter Park, FL 32789.

CHAPTER SEVEN
Contracts

■ CONTRACTS ARE A LEGAL and practical necessity in every business. I cannot cover the entire field of contract law here, but I'll discuss some of the fundamentals, so that you'll be aware of what you need to know to protect your art gallery or craft retail business.

What Is a Contract?

A contract is a legally binding promise or set of promises between two or more parties. The parties can be either individuals or business organizations. If one or more of the parties fails to perform the promise or promises made by contract—usually called a breach—the law will provide remedies to the injured party.

The three basic elements of every contract are the offer, the acceptance, and the consideration. For example, a salesperson shows a customer an oil painting at your gallery and suggests that she buy it (this is the offer). The customer says she likes the painting and wants to buy it (the acceptance). They agree on a price (the consideration). This is the basic framework of a contract, but there are a great many variations on the theme.

Implied Contracts

You enter into many contracts without thinking much about them—for example, the telephone company agrees to provide telecommunication services with the understanding that you promise to pay for those services under certain agreed-upon terms. Likewise, if you order three limited edition prints from an artist, the promise to pay is implied in the order, and is enforceable when the prints are delivered.

With implied contracts, however, things can often become sticky. For example, suppose an art show promoter asks you for a supply of posters by an artist whose work you have just begun publishing. You deliver several dozen. The promoter disposes of all the posters you send, and is overheard commenting that it is the most attractive and best-quality poster he has ever handled. Is there an implied contract to purchase in this arrangement? That may depend on whether you are normally in the business of giving away free samples of newly published posters. It would have been wiser for you to clearly specify the terms under which you were providing the posters, either orally or in writing.

Express Contracts

An express contract is one in which all the details are spelled out. For example, you might make a contract with a potter for six dozen hand-thrown mugs to be delivered to you on October 1, at a price of $3 per mug, to be paid within 30 days of receipt. This is fairly straightforward. If either party fails to live up to any material part of the contract, there has been a breach of contract. The other party may withhold performance of his or her obligation until receiving assurance that the breaching party will perform. If no assurance is received, the aggrieved party may have a cause of action for breach of contract.

If you had advertised availability of the mugs during the week of October 1, but the mugs were delivered on October 15, time was an important consideration, and you would not be required to accept the late shipment. But if time were not a material consideration, the potter, even with the slight delay, has substantially complied with the terms of the contract, and you would have to accept the delivery. Therefore, it's important to clearly identify those terms that are material to the contract.

Oral and Written Contracts

Implied contracts are usually oral; express contracts can be either oral or written. The best practice is always to get it in writing, particularly for those contracts you enter into on a regular basis that are critical to the viability and smooth running of your business.

Many gallery owners and craft retailers prefer to do business strictly on the basis of a handshake, particularly with their artists and customers. With a handshake agreement, the assumption is that the business relationship is based upon mutual trust alone. Although there may be some validity to this, far too many trusting business people have suffered adverse consequences because of their idealistic reliance upon the sanctity of oral contracts.

Even in the best business relationships, one or both parties might simply forget the precise details of the original oral agreement. Memories do fade. Or both parties might have quite different perceptions about the terms of the agreement reached. When the agreement is put into writing, however, there is much less doubt as to the terms of the arrangement (although even a written contract may contain ambiguities if it is not drafted with considerable care).

Contracts are enforceable only if they can be proven. Proof of oral contracts relies on the testimony of the parties involved. If one of the parties is not able to establish by a preponderance of evidence that his or her version of the contract is the correct one, the oral contract may be considered nonexistent—as though it had never been made. It is a truism that oral contracts are not worth the paper they are written on.

The function of a written contract, therefore, is not only to make very clear the understanding of the parties regarding the agreement and terms of the contract, but also to prove that there is an agreement and contract.

In addition, in some states, in order to be valid, the sale of editioned prints or other multiples must be accompanied by disclosure documents prescribed by statute.

Case Study

Let's evaluate these potential business situations for the hypothetical gallery owner Pat Smith to determine which arrangments constitute contracts and which are enforceable.

Smith is a gallery owner who has an impressive portfolio of work by the noted artist Pablo Picarro. At a cocktail party, Mr. Jones expresses to Smith an interest in Picarro's art. "It looks like the market value of Picarro paintings keeps going up," Jones tells Smith. "I'm going to buy one while I can still afford it."

Is this an enforceable oral contract? Does it meet the three criteria of a contract: offer, acceptance, and consideration? What are the terms of the offer—has a price been specified for a particular painting? No, Jones has not made a specific offer that Smith can accept. He has simply expressed an opinion and a vague expression of intent.

Ms. Brown offers to pay Smith $4,000 for a Picarro sculpture that she saw at Smith's gallery several weeks ago. At the gallery, it was listed at $4,500, but Smith agrees to accept the lower price.

Is this an enforceable contract? Yes! Brown has offered to pay a specific amount for a specific piece, and Smith has accepted the offer. This is a binding, express, oral contract.

34

One day Jones shows up at Smith's gallery and sees a particular print for which he offers $1,000. Smith accepts and promises to deliver a bill of sale and an appropriate print disclosure form the next week, at which time Jones will pay for the print. An hour later, Brown shows up. She likes the same print and offers Smith $1,500 for it. Can Smith accept the later offer?

No. A contract already exists with Jones. An offer was made and accepted. The fact that the object has not yet been delivered or paid for does not make the contract any less binding.

Mr. Green discusses the kind of frame he would like Smith to put on a particular photograph Smith has just acquired. He offers to pay $5,000 for the photo if the final product is satisfactory to him. Green approves the framing and the matting material, and Smith completes the work. But Green refuses to accept the framed photo because it is not satisfactory to him.

Green's offer was conditional upon his satisfaction with the completed work. Smith understood that he would receive payment only if he produced something that met Green's subjective standards—a risky way to do business. In this situation, there is no enforceable contract between Smith and Green.

Suppose, instead, that Green arrives at Smith's gallery and agrees that the framed photo is satisfactory. When Smith delivers the photo, however, Green says he has changed his mind and refuses to accept it. In this case, Green has breached his contract. The oral contract became binding at the moment he indicated the framed work met his conditions.

Statute of Frauds

The Statute of Frauds was designed to prevent fraud and perjury. According to this statute, there are at least two types of contracts that must be in writing if they are to be legally enforceable: (1) any contract that, by its terms, cannot be completed in less than one year; and (2) any contract

that involves the sale of goods for over $500. This rule is narrowly interpreted, so if there is any possibility, no matter how remote, that the contract could be fully performed within one year, the contract need not be in writing.

For example, if a jeweler agreed to submit one piece of custom-designed jewelry to a craft retailer each year for a period of five years, the contract would have to be in writing because, by the very terms of the agreement, there is no way the contract could be performed within one year. If, on the other hand, the contract called for the jeweler to deliver five pieces within a period of five years, the contract would not have to be in writing to be enforceable, because it is possible, although perhaps not probable, that the jeweler could deliver all five pieces within the first year.

The Statute of Frauds, as set forth in Article 2 of the Uniform Commercial Code (UCC), further provides that any contract for the sale of goods valued at $500 or more is not enforceable unless it has been put into writing and signed by the party against whom enforcement is being sought. (The law defines goods as all things that are movable at the time of making the contract except for the money used as payment.)

Smith's sale to Green was for both goods and services, but because the goods involved were over $500 in value, the contract should have been in writing to ensure enforceability. If, however, the contract had been one of performance of personal services only—say, for framing performed by Smith using Green's materials—the UCC would not apply, and the contract would be enforceable whether or not it was in writing.

The fact that a contract for a price in excess of $500 is not in writing does not void the agreement or render it illegal. The parties are free to perform the oral arrangement, but if one party refuses to perform, the other will be unable to legally require performance of the agreement.

The real question becomes whether a particular contract involves the sale of goods for a price of $500 or more. For example, if a potter agrees to provide a craft retailer with all its pottery inventory for the coming year—whatever that may be—how is the price to be determined? Or, if a jeweler sells a number of pieces to a gallery where the total purchase price exceeds $500 but the price of the individual works is less than $500, which price governs? In light of these possible ambiguities, the safest course is to put all contracts in writing.

No-Cost Written Agreements

You may feel you do not have the time, energy, or patience to draft contracts. After all, you're in business to sell art or craft works, not to formulate written contracts steeped in legal jargon. You may find that a supplier, artist, or craftsperson is willing to draft a satisfactory contract for you—but that's not very likely! Be wary of signing any form contracts: They will almost invariably be one-sided, with all terms in favor of whomever paid to have them drafted.

As an alternative, you can hire an attorney to draft contracts for you. This might be worthwhile for substantial transactions, but for smaller ones, the legal fees may offset the benefits derived from having a written contract.

The UCC offers businesses a third and perhaps the best alternative: you needn't draft any contract or rely on anyone else to do so. The UCC provides that, where both parties are merchants and one party sends to the other a written confirmation of an oral contract within a reasonable time after that contract was made, and the recipient does not object to the confirming memorandum within ten days of its receipt, the contract will be deemed enforceable. A merchant is defined as any person who normally deals in goods of the kind sold or who, because of occupation, represents herself or himself as having knowledge or skill peculiar to the practices or goods involved in the transaction.

When an agreement is based on written confirmation rather than a contract, however, neither party can use the Statute of Frauds as a defense, assuming that the recipient fails to object within ten days after receipt. The party sending the confirming memorandum must still prove that an oral contract was, in fact, made prior to or at the same time as the written confirmation. But once such proof is offered, neither party can raise the Statute of Frauds to avoid enforcement of the agreement, because this is a specific exception to that law.

The advantage of the confirming memorandum over a written contract lies in the fact that the confirming memorandum can be used without the active participation of the other contracting party. It would suffice, for example, to simply state: "This memorandum is to confirm our oral agreement." But it would be useful to provide a bit more detail in the confirming memorandum, such as the subject of the contract, the date it was made, and the price or other consideration to be paid.

You might draft something like the following:

This memorandum is to confirm our oral agreement made on July 3, 1992, in which you [craft artist] agreed to deliver to me [craft retailer] on or before September 19, 1992, three weavings, each approximately 2' x 2' in earth tones, for the purchase price of $600 each.

The advantages of providing detail in the confirming memorandum are twofold. First, in the event of a dispute, you could introduce the memorandum as proof of the terms of the oral agreement. And second, the recipient of the memorandum (and, for that matter, the party sending the memorandum) will not be able to claim any terms of contract other than those contained in the memorandum. For example, the retailer in the preceding example would not be able to claim at some point that the contract called for delivery of four weavings, because the quantity was clearly stated in the written memo and was not objected to by the artist.

The retailer, however, could testify that the oral contract required the weaver to use synthetic fiber instead of natural fiber, because this testimony would not be inconsistent with the terms stated in the memorandum. To prevent either party from adding or inventing terms that are not spelled out in the confirming memorandum, the memorandum should end with a clause requiring all other provisions to be contained in a written and signed document. For example:

This is the entire agreement between the parties and no modification, alteration, or additional terms shall be enforceable unless in writing and signed by both parties.

Essentials of the Written Contract

A contract rarely need be—or should be—a long, complicated document written in legal jargon designed to provide a handsome income to lawyers. Indeed, a contract should be written in simple language that both parties can understand, and should spell out the terms of the agreement.

The contract should include:

1. The date of the agreement.

2. Identification of the parties—the buyer and seller in the case of sale of goods or services.

3. A description of the goods or services sold.

4. Price or other consideration.

5. The signatures of the parties involved.

In addition to these basics, the agreement should spell out whatever other terms might be applicable: pricing arrangements, payment schedules, insurance coverage, consignment details, and so forth (see Chapter 8). A written document that leaves out essential terms of the contract presents many of the same problems of proof and ambiguity as an oral contract. Contract terms should be well conceived, clearly drafted, legible, and in plain English so that all the parties can easily read and understand them.

For some useful form contracts to refer to, see *Business and Legal Forms (In Plain English)® for Craftspeople*, 2d. ed., 1993, Interweave Press, and *The Deskbook of Art Law*, 2d. ed., Vol. 3, Oceana Publishing Co., 1993.

CHAPTER EIGHT
Dealing with Artists, Craftspeople, and Other Suppliers

■ UNLESS YOU INTEND TO MARKET only works you create, you will need to establish business relationships with artists, craftspeople, and other suppliers. If you have significant capital, you may be willing to purchase artwork outright and accept the risk that you may not sell it. This arrangement is common in Europe's fine art galleries and throughout much of its craft industry. In the United States, however, it is more common for artists to consign their works for sale to arts and craft galleries.

Consignment

In consignment relationships, the artist or craftsperson retains ownership of the work until it is sold. The gallery owner or crafts retailer promotes and handles the sale of the work and receives a portion of the sales price as a commission.

Artists and those who sell art usually view their relationship as a personal one—more like a marriage than a business venture. This sentiment generally results in a vague business relationship with the specific terms rarely put in writing. Unfortunately, like the modern marriage, the relationship between dealer and artist may eventually sour. As I stressed in Chapter 7, without a written agreement, either party may find itself injured and without a remedy.

Recognizing the many potential problems inherent in the relationship between dealer and artist, most states have enacted consignment statutes (see p. 120), modeled after New York's statute. New York was the first to adopt a consignment statute designed to protect unwary artists from unscrupulous dealers. The law characterizes the relationship between the artist and dealer as principal and agent rather than debtor and creditor. This means that the artist retains title to the work; the dealer sells the work on behalf of the artist and holds proceeds from the sale in trust for the artist.

Regardless of whether the contract between them is written or oral, dealers' and artists' relationships are subject to the Uniform Commercial Code (UCC), which fills in contractual gaps and interprets the intent of the parties when disputes arise. Typically, those states with consignment statutes have exempted the relationship between dealers and artists from the UCC regulation that allows the dealer's creditors access to goods held on consignment. In many states, the dealer's creditors cannot attach an artist's consigned work or the proceeds from its sale, even if the dealer files bankruptcy, because both the artwork and the money are being held in trust.

Consignment statutes are designed to establish rules between the parties and, in some instances, to require written contracts. Some permit the parties to vary terms, while others mandate rigid adherence. For example, the New York statute permits the artist who is entitled to be paid on an installment sale to waive receipt of full payment before the dealer may retain any installments, provided that the waiver is in writing and that the artist receives the first $2,500 of installment payments within a 12-month period. The California statute, on the other hand, prohibits any sort of waiver of the artist's rights.

Exclusivity

It is quite common for galleries and craft retailers to insist upon an exclusivity arrangement when contracting to market the works of an artist or craftsperson. Such an arrangement might specify exclusive right to sell all of the artist's work within a particular geographical area, for example, or it may permit the sale of only certain of the artist's works. In exchange for the artist's grant of exclusivity, the gallery agrees to diligently promote and sell the artist's work. Occasionally, artists will demand minimum sales guarantees as a condition of the continued grant of exclusivity.

A common dispute in exclusivity arrangements is the meaning of exclusive. Similar to the relationship of agent and seller in real estate transactions, the relationship between the dealer and artist may be characterized as either an "exclusive agent" relationship or an "exclusive power to sell" relationship. In an exclusive agent relationship, the dealer is the sole agent allowed to sell the artist's work. Under these terms, artists can sell their own works from their studios and owe the dealer nothing, because no agent was involved in the sale. In an exclusive power to sell relationship, any time an artist's work is sold, whether or not from the gallery or retail shop of the dealer, the artist owes the dealer a commission. The dealer takes the position that he or she is entitled to this commission, especially when representing an unknown artist, because the capital and effort expended in promoting the artist may indirectly have resulted in the sale of the work.

While the relationship may seem as simple as the promise of a gallery owner or craft retailer to sell an artist's or craftperson's work in exchange for a commission, rarely is the arrangement so elementary. Exclusivity arrangements are quite controversial because of numerous issues that are difficult to clarify. How are the geographical areas defined, for example? By ZIP code, municipal boundaries, commercial zones? Sometimes a single building has its own ZIP code. Artists and craftspeople also often feel that exclusivity arrangements deprive them of sales. The definition of "sale", for the purpose of the arrangement, is also subject to interpretation. Is a charitable donation to a museum, for example, considered a "sale"? What about bartering?

An exclusivity arrangement should be developed in detail, in order to clarify as many of these potentially ambiguous issues as possible. The parties should consider all questions that may arise during the relationship, negotiate how these situations will be handled should they arise, and create a written contract with provisions that represent their understanding.

The contract should answer at least these basic questions:

1. Who are the parties?

2. Is the dealer an individual or an organization?

3. Must the dealer remain at a particular location?

4. Can the dealer assign rights to another dealer?

5. Does the artist's surviving spouse or children have any rights under the contract should the artist die?

6. What will happen if the artist incorporates?

7. What is the contract's specific term? What are the conditions and methods of termination? Is the relationship dependent upon a certain number of successful sales by the dealer, or production of a certain number of works by the artist?

8. Who pays for insurance?

9. Who is responsible for packing and shipping? If the work is not all sold when the contract terminates, who is responsible for storage until the artist has reclaimed the work? Who pays for shipping and storage?

10. Who pays for framing and, if the work does not sell, who owns the frame?

11. What are the artist's rights with respect to copyright and reproductions?

12. When and how is the artist to be paid, and in what currency?

13. If the sale is an installment sale, who is paid first, the artist or the gallery owner?

Many of these items are expressly dealt with in state consignment statutes. You should work with an attorney experienced in art and craft law to determine whether you are subject to such statutes, their requirements, and whether or not they are modifiable by contract. For more information on the types of business concerns you might want to address in your contract, see *The Craft Business Encyclopedia* by Michael Scott, rev. ed. (San Diego, Calif.: Harcourt Brace Jovanovich, 1993).

Returning to the marriage analogy, a "prenuptial agreement" between the dealer and artist need not injure the personal relationship they enjoy, but may be the only protection they have if the honeymoon ends. (For a sample artist-gallery consignment contract, see p. 121.)

Artist's Rights

There are numerous state and federal laws enacted for the purpose of encouraging artists to feel secure when exercising their creative abilities. You should be aware of these laws and the limitations they may impose on your relationship with artists and craftspeople and those to whom you sell. Carefully examine all contracts between you and those from whom you acquire the work you are selling to determine whether there are any contractual limitations or obligations on you or your customers.

Resale Royalties

There are often specific legal and contractual obligations when a gallery or craft retailer is reselling a work, for example, when selling a piece procured from a private collection rather than directly from the artist or craftsperson. In Europe, often the law requires those who resell art to pay a certain amount from the resale to the artist or the artist's estate. The amount of this payment—called a resale royalty—varies from country to country, and the laws customarily impose the obligation only on sales that take place within that country.

The United States does not yet have a national resale royalties law, although the Visual Artists Rights Act of 1990 may signal a change. Under that law, the National Endowment for the Arts was required to conduct a survey on the desirability of such a law and present its findings to Congress. The report, presented in late 1992, was inconclusive and it's likely that additional studies will be conducted before any definitive recommendation is made.

The first jurisdiction in the United States to enact a resale royalty law was the City of Seattle. That law provides that, when the City resells any artwork it acquires as part of its Art in Public Places program, a resale royalty is to be paid to the artist or the artist's estate, provided that a current address for the beneficiary is on file with the City.

The State of California has the only statewide resale royalties law. It provides that, whenever a work of fine art is sold and the seller resides in California or the sale takes place in California, the seller or the seller's agent shall pay 5% of the amount of such sale to the artist of such work of fine art, or to the artist's estate.

The California law has been the subject of numerous discussions and is still the principal prototype in the United States. For the purposes of the statute, an artist is defined as the person who created the art and who is, at the time of resale, either a citizen of the United States or has resided in California for a minimum of two years. Fine art is defined as "an original painting, sculpture, or drawing, or an original work of art in glass." The act does not apply to the initial sale of a work of fine art where the legal title to the work is vested in the artist, to the resale of a work of fine art for a gross sales price (or fair market value of property, including art taken in trade) of less than $1,000, or to the resale of the work for a gross price less than the purchase price paid by the seller. Also excluded from the act are sales that occur more than 20 years after the artist's death, resales of works by an art dealer to a purchaser within 10 years of the initial sale of the work by the artist to the dealer, provided all intervening sales are between dealers, and to sales of works of stained glass artistry where the work has been permanently attached to real property and is sold as part of the sale of the real property to which it is attached.

Generally, the responsibility for paying the artist is with the seller but, when a work of fine art is sold at an auction or by a gallery, dealer, broker, museum, or other person acting as the seller's agent, the agent must withhold the 5%, locate and pay the artist, or pay the artist's estate. If the artist cannot be located within 90 days, the royalty is transferred to the California State Arts Council. The Arts Council then must attempt to locate the artist. If the artist still cannot be located and if the artist does not file a written claim for the money within seven years from the date of the sale, the money becomes the property of the Arts Council for use in acquiring fine art for its Art in Public Places Program.

Many artists and craftspeople have established their own resale royalty arrangement by contractually requiring purchasers to pay a specified amount should the purchaser resell the work. Determine whether any work you are selling is subject to a resale royalty and whether you or the person with whom you are dealing has any resale royalty obligations. Check your contract with the supplier, artist, or collector and any prior contracts they may have had regarding the piece to determine whether you or the purchaser may have some ongoing financial obligation to the artist or the artist's estate. You may also wish to obtain a representation or warranty regarding any ongoing royalty obligations.

Moral Rights

The unique relationship between an artist or craftsperson and the work created has given rise to a collection of rights known in Europe as the droit moral (moral rights). The notion began in France and spread to more than 80 countries. It is embodied in the Bern Copyright Treaty (see Chapter 12), to which the United States is a signatory. These rights are intended to provide the creative person with additional incentives for the creative act by protecting the integrity of the work and its creator's reputation. These moral rights include the right to create, the right of disclosure (i.e., to decide when the work is ready to be displayed), the right to withdraw (i.e., to remove a defaced work from display), the right to name attribution, and the right to preserve the integrity of a work.

Federal moral rights—In the United States, the Visual Artists Rights Act of 1990 (VARA) contains many elements of the European droit moral. It applies to any work of art that is "a painting, drawing, print, or sculpture, existing in a single copy, or limited edition of 200 or fewer, signed and consecutively numbered," and to photographic images produced for exhibition purposes only as signed, numbered editions of 200 or fewer.

Among the rights protected by VARA is the right of paternity. The artist or craftsperson is allowed to claim "authorship" of a work he or she created. The artist or craftsperson also has the right "to prevent the use of his or her name as the author of the work of visual art in the event of distortion, mutilation, or other modification of the work which could be prejudicial to his or her honor or reputation."

An artist or craftsperson ordinarily may not object to the use of his or her name in a truthful statement that he or she created the work or that the work is based on or derived from his or her work in the absence of contractual provisions to the contrary. Similarly, the omission of an artist's or craftsperson's name from his or her work ordinarily is not actionable unless the omission amounts to a breach of contract, or the work is covered by VARA or a state moral rights law. (For a list of state moral rights laws, see p. 143.)

Artists and craftspeople also have some rights to prevent their works from being altered, distorted, or destroyed. VARA is careful to exclude from prohibition any "modification resulting from passage of time or the inherent nature of the materials" and "any modification which is the result of conservation, or of the public presentation, including lighting and placement of the work . . . unless caused by gross negligence."

The law also provides artists and craftspeople the right to "prevent any destruction of a work of recognized stature." The question of what constitutes "a work of recognized stature" is determined, on a case-by-case basis, by the expert testimony of scholars, curators, gallery owners, crafts retailers, and presumably, collectors.

State moral rights—Several states have enacted statutes that protect the moral right of integrity. The California Act prohibits anyone, except an artist who owns and possesses the work he created, to intentionally deface, mutilate, alter, or destroy a work of fine art. The act also provides that no person who frames, conserves, or restores a work of art shall deface, mutilate, alter, or destroy the work by any act constituting gross negligence.

Under the New York Act, the artist may bring an action for "just and valid reason" to prevent his or her name from appearing on or in connection with a work of fine art. "Just and valid reason" would include situations where the work of fine art has been altered, defaced, mutilated, or modified other than by the artist, and damage to the artist's reputation is reasonably likely to occur or has already occurred as a result. New York also prohibits any unauthorized person from publicly displaying, publishing, or reproducing an altered work of fine art that is represented as the work of the artist or under such circumstances in which the work would reasonably be regarded as being the work of the artist, and thereby possibly damage the artist's reputation.

Like the California statute, the New York legislation provides an exemption for bona fide conservation, unless the conservator is negligent in performing the work. New York also provides that alterations resulting from the passage of time or from the inherent nature of the materials are not covered, again unless resulting from gross negli-

gence. Changes in works prepared under contract for advertising or trade use are not violations of the act, unless the contract so provides.

As with resale royalties, gallery owners and crafts retailers should carefully examine contracts between themselves and those from whom the work they sell is acquired, as well as any prior contracts, to determine whether there are any contractual limitations imposed on the dealer or which should be disclosed to the purchaser. VARA, state laws, and supplier contracts may all impose obligations on you and your customers. Care should be taken to be aware of these items.

Import Issues

There are a number of issues you need to consider before importing art or craft into the United States for sale in your gallery or shop.

First, you should determine whether the item you desire to import has been legally exported. Many antiquities, for example, may not be removed from the country of origin or from a country in which they have resided for so long as to become a "national treasure". The law in this area is quite complex, and you need also to comply with the conditions of treaties such as the UNESCO Convention on the Means of Prohibiting and Preventing the Illicit Import, Export, and Transfer of Ownership of Cultural Property. In addition, transporting certain items—such as, for example, pre-Columbian art—over state lines or national boundaries, may subject the transporter or others involved in the arrangement to criminal liability when the country from which the item was taken has declared its ownership of those items. You should work with an experienced art lawyer when dealing with antiquities.

Customs duties are usually imposed on commodities imported into the United States, but works of art may enter the United States duty free. It is, therefore, essential to determine what is "art" for customs purposes. The law in this area is also quite complex, but there are some guidelines.

1. In order for an item to quality as duty-free fine art, it cannot be functional. Therefore, most crafts do not qualify.

2. The work must be created by an artist and cannot be imported for the purpose of commercialization—for example, you cannot import a duty-free painting to be used as cover art on a magazine.

3. Fine art prints can enter duty free only if they are hand pulled from handmade plates.

4. Only the first 12 pieces of sculptured limited editions can enter the United States as duty-free art.

There are numerous other technical qualifications that have evolved from legal cases and special-interest legislation. For example, functional crafts are generally not considered art, but may still enjoy duty-free treatment under a special customs law known as the Generalized System of Preferences (GSP). This law was enacted to provide certain underdeveloped countries with the ability to have some of their commodities enter the United States without the imposition of tariffs. The countries on the GSP list change quite regularly, as do the duty-free commodities. It, therefore, is essential for you to consult with a customs broker and/or an experienced art lawyer when contemplating overseas purchasing. Interestingly, with the exception of certain Native American items, there is no restriction on the export of art from the United States.

Native American Works

Art dealers and craft retailers who handle Native American works should be aware of the several laws that pertain to the sale of these items, such as the Native American Graves and Repatriation Act of 1990 and the Indian Arts and Crafts Act of 1935, as amended in 1990.

The Repatriation Act bans any trade in human remains and restricts the trade of certain other cultural items. There are possible penalties of fines and up to a year in prison. The Arts and Crafts Act created the Indian Arts and Crafts Board as an agency under the Secretary of the Interior. The Board has adopted a certification mark, which may be used by Native Americans to identify their newly created work. Civil and criminal penalties may be imposed for counterfeiting the Board's marks and misrepresenting works as the creations of Indian artists; there has not, however, been a single prosecution under the Act. The Board is also authorized to assist tribes and individual Indian artists in obtaining registration of their trademarks free of charge.

Michigan, New York, New Mexico, and Alaska have enacted laws for the purpose of inhibiting counterfeit Indian art from being passed off as authentic work created by Native American artists. In some of these statutes, for example, New Mexico's, a duty is imposed on the dealer to make "due inquiry" in order to determine whether items represented to be created by Native Americans are, in fact, made by individuals who can legally make that claim.

You should, therefore, become familiar with the federal and state laws regulating Native American Art, crafts, and other cultural property if your gallery or crafts retail shop deals in these items. Here, too, working with an experienced art lawyer will be important.

Price Antidiscrimination

Congress has enacted legislation to prevent unfair price discrimination in the sale of commodities such as art or crafts in interstate commerce: that is, sales across state lines or those likely to affect someone in another state.

Gallery owners and crafts retailers and their suppliers are free to choose to whom they will and will not sell, but, according to The Robinson-Patman Act, they cannot discriminate against buyers by charging different prices for identical items sold at nearly the same time without a good business reason. The Robinson-Patman Act also controls whether a supplier of merchandise (such as an artist or craftsperson) can refuse to deal with a customer (such as a gallery or retailer), accord or deny special concessions and benefits to a customer, or sell only on the condition that the customer maintain a certain resale price structure.

A violation of the Act can occur under three conditions: First, as injury to a seller, if one seller attempts to price a competing seller out of business. Second, as injury to the buyer, if a seller charges different prices to different buyers who then compete with each other in the same market. Third, as injury at the customer level, if a seller prices a work so that the ultimate consumer may pay less in one case than the other.

The Act does not allow the paying of brokerage fees or provision of merchandising allowances or services to a favored buyer. Under the Sherman Antitrust Act, a seller cannot control the buyer's resale pricing. In other words, the artist, craftsperson, or supplier can neither sell to a gallery at a price so low as to injure a competing gallery's business nor cause injury to a gallery by imposing resale conditions that would hamper the gallery's competitiveness in the marketplace. In addition to preventing an artist, craftsperson, or supplier from discriminating against retailers, Robinson-Patman also prohibits a retailer from accepting low prices or other benefits that may injure a fellow retailer's competitiveness.

The Robinson-Patman provisions are enforced primarily by the Federal Trade Commission. The Department of Justice may also enforce Robinson-Patman prohibitions in conjunction with other antitrust actions against a probable violator. Perhaps the most effective enforcement may be private suits brought by disgruntled galleries or crafts retailers against a discriminatory artist, craftsperson, or other supplier. Such suits may avoid the bureaucratic backlog of government enforcement and involve the actual parties, which likely will result in more accurate and timely punishment for wrongdoing. Additionally, injured parties may be awarded triple damages and attorneys' fees.

Some states have enacted legislation similar to Robinson-Patman to prevent price discrimination in intrastate commerce.

CHAPTER NINE
Catalog Sales

■ SELLING THROUGH CATALOGS provides art gallery and craft shop owners with an opportunity to expand their markets. There are a number of ways to take advantage of catalog sales: by printing and distributing a catalog featuring your inventory; by pooling resources with others to produce a cooperative catalog; or by offering your items in somebody else's catalog.

Creating Your Own Catalog

Publishing and distributing a catalog is, in essence, starting a new business. You should have a business plan, which includes an estimate of the total cost of the project—for example, the costs of photography, typography or desktop publishing, printing, binding, and mailing. Those who sell by direct mail also need to identify those to whom catalogs should be sent. For this, it is best to enlist the aid of a list broker, who specializes in evaluating and managing lists of names for direct-mail marketing. A broker will customize and personalize mailing lists according to your specific needs. Once you have begun mailing, the lists must be kept "clean," which means keeping names and addresses current and periodically removing the names of those who have not been buying. Gallery owners and crafts retailers should include regular customers on the list and collect, whenever possible, the names and addresses of visitors and browsers who wish to be on the mailing list.

Federal trade commission regulations—The Federal Trade Commission (FTC) regulates the sale of merchandise through mail orders. Be-cause of the numerous problems consumers have had with mail-order companies, the FTC is quite active in policing the market. Many of its rules deal with the availability of merchandise, shipping dates, price variations, and the like. Failure to comply with these technical rules will be deemed an unfair trade practice, possibly subjecting the catalog merchandiser to FTC sanctions, such as injunctive relief and damages.

There are some interesting legal issues related to catalog selling. For example, an ad in a catalog is not considered an offer to sell the object depicted for the price designated; rather, it is considered an invitation for offers that may or may not be accepted by the advertiser. This is important, because it means that you are not obligated to sell the work for the price specified if it becomes necessary for you to change the price. Be sure to prominently note in the ad that the price may be subject to change. It is not good business practice to advertise one price and actually charge a higher price. In fact, it may be unlawful to do this on a regular basis. The practice of promoting an item for one price but discouraging its purchase and selling higher-priced items, referred to as "bait-and-switch", is unlawful under most state laws as consumer fraud.

Because many works of art or craft are unique or created in limited quantities, it is unlikely that the exact piece shown in your advertisement will be available for every purchaser. Make it clear that the prospective purchaser will probably be getting something substantially similar to the item advertised, but not necessarily identical. Although there is no legal obligation to make purchasers aware of these potential inconsistencies, being fair generates goodwill.

Under FTC rules, when an ad is put into a catalog, the seller must have a reasonable basis to believe that the goods can be shipped within any time stated in the ad, but in no event shall this period be longer than 30 days. This means that you must have inventory on hand when the catalog is distributed or, at the very least, have ready access to the items depicted.

If it is necessary to revise a shipping date, you must have a reasonable basis for believing that you can deliver the merchandise on that new date, and you should inform the buyer. If the revised date for shipping the merchandise is within 30 days from the original scheduled shipping date, you must notify the buyer that the buyer will be deemed to have consented to the delay unless the buyer objects in writing. (FTC rules require the seller to provide the buyer with adequate means of notifying the seller of any consent to a delay—either a postcard or stamped, self-addressed envelope.)

If it is impossible to predict exactly when the goods will be shipped, and the buyer is informed of this fact as well as the reason for your inability to predict the new shipping date, then the FTC will not object to your failure to ship the item within the revised period. You must, however, offer the buyer the option to either consent to a further delay or to cancel the order and receive a prompt refund.

If the revised shipping date is more than 30 days from the original date the goods were to be shipped, or if you cannot provide a precise revised shipping date, then you must notify the buyer that the order will automatically be canceled unless you are able to ship within 30 days from the original shipping date or unless you receive written notification from the purchaser that the purchaser will consent to a later or indefinite shipping date. You must also notify the buyer that the buyer may cancel the order at any time until the goods actually are shipped. This is true even where the buyer has consented in writing to the delay.

If you are still unable to ship the merchandise on the revised shipping date, then you must give the buyer a revised option either to extend the date of shipment or cancel the order.

Cooperative Cataloging

Cooperative cataloging provides the gallery with all of the advantages of catalog advertizing while allowing it to share the costs with other galleries. The larger volume of the catalog may in fact bring down cost. In addition, the catalog may give all the participants wider exposure to markets they would not ordinarily have.

You should be careful to determine whether any of the other co-op members are in competition with you before entering into a cooperative venture. A co-op is a firm of partnership, so you can work a fair distribution of costs among yourselves. If the other members of the co-op do not fulfill their obligations, however, you may wind up having to pay all of the expenses. (See Chapter 1 for a discussion of partnerships.)

Selling through Someone Else's Catalog

If a gallery owner or crafts retailer sells work to a catalog company, the FTC rules would apply only to the catalog company not to the retailer. There are, however, other risks for the retailer to keep in mind.

If, for example, the catalog carries a piece that is not delivered by the gallery or shop to the catalog company in accordance with the contractual obligation between the gallery and catalog company, then the gallery or shop may be exposed to liability for breach of contract with the catalog company. In most instances, however, courts will not award damages to the catalog company for lost sales, because it is almost impossible to prove with any accuracy the amount of sales one would have had if the contract had been properly performed. If the catalog company actually has sales that must be rescinded because a gallery or shop did not deliver merchandise when promised, the catalog company will be able to specify the amount of sales lost and the amount of other expenses incurred as a result of the breach. Similarly, a gallery or shop that delivers nonconforming works to the catalog company may also be liable for breach of contract. Here, too, the amount of damage caused by the breach will be more easily established if the catalog company is actually in possession of orders that have been rescinded.

Crafts retailers and gallery owners who offer items through catalogs will be relieved to know that, in 1992, the Supreme Court upheld its historical interpretation of state sales tax codes. Under the ruling, catalog merchants are required to collect the sales tax from customers residing in the company's home state or in any state where the company has a physical presence, such as a branch shop or a warehouse. Sales tax need not be collected from customers in states other than the one in which the catalog company is located or has a substantial presence.

CHAPTER TEN
People Who Work for You

■ THERE COMES A TIME in the life of almost every art gallery or craft retail business when it is necessary to get help, be it brain or brawn. The first type of help most commonly needed is a bookkeeper or accountant who can handle taxes, payables, and the like. As things get a little hectic around the shop or gallery, you might then hire someone to help with packing, unpacking, or running errands. If selling is not your greatest talent, you may engage the services of a salesperson. If this salesperson is really good, you will soon have to hire more employees to keep up with the demand.

Independent Contractors

If you hire a bookkeeper or accountant to go over your records once or twice a year, that person is most likely an independent contractor. An independent contractor is a person hired on a one-time or job-by-job basis. Although paid for their services by the hiring firm or individual, contractors are their own bosses and may even employ others to do the work for them.

You may need to provide some independent contractors with your "trade secrets" for purposes of assisting with your business. Be sure to include a provision in your contract with them that restricts the contractor's use or disclosure of your trade secrets without your prior written permission.

The fact that the person is independent, and not your employee, means that you do not have to pay social security, withhold income taxes, provide workers' compensation coverage, or comply with the myriad rules imposed on employers. More important, you are generally not liable for injuries to a third party resulting from the independent contractor's negligence or wrongful acts, even while working for you. However, there are basic types of situations where, despite your innocence, an independent contractor can render you legally responsible for his or her wrongful acts:

1. If an employer is careless in hiring an independent contractor—that is, if a careful investigation would have disclosed facts to indicate that the contractor was not qualified—the employer may be liable when the independent contractor fails to properly perform the job.

2. If a job is so dangerous as to be characterized as ultrahazardous (a legal term) and is to be performed for the employer's benefit, then, regardless of who performs the work, the employer remains legally responsible for any injuries that occur during the performance of the work. Thus, an art or craft gallery desiring to have a fireworks display for a grand opening cannot escape liability by having independent contractors light the fuses or aim the rockets.

3. An employer may be required by law to perform certain tasks for the health and safety of the community. These responsibilities are said to be nondelegable—that is, an employer cannot delegate them and thus escape liability for their improper performance. If, therefore, a nondelegable duty is performed by an independent contractor, the employer will remain responsible for any injury that results. A good

example of a nondelegable duty is compliance with the law (common in many states) that home owners and business owners are responsible for keeping their sidewalks free of dangerous obstacles. If a business owner hires an independent contractor to fulfill this obligation by removing ice during the winter, the business owner is still legally liable if someone is injured on the slippery sidewalk, even if the accident resulted from the contractor's carelessness. Another example of a nondelegable duty is found in the tax laws. A business owner is obligated to file an accurate return and pay the appropriate tax. The fact that an underpayment resulted from the carelessness of a CPA, who is an independent contractor, will not relieve the business owner from liability to the government. The business owner may be able to recover any penalties and interest from the careless CPA.

Employees

The second capacity in which someone can work for you is as an employee. This category includes anyone over whose work you exercise direct control—helpers, apprentices, salespeople who represent you alone, a bookkeeper who is a member of your staff, and so forth. The formation of this relationship entails nothing more than an agreement on your side to hire someone, and an agreement by that person to work for you. Although a written contract is not necessary except in the case of employment for more than one year, I suggest that employment terms be put down in writing, so that there is no misunderstanding later.

Employment Contracts

There must be a written contract specifying the term of employment if it will be longer than one year; otherwise, either party may terminate the relationship at any time. There is no prescribed form that the contract must take, but there are certain items that should be considered.

The first is the term of employment. An employment contract may be either terminable at will or of a fixed duration. A contract that specifies a fixed period gives the employee some job security and creates a moral and contractual obligation for the employee to remain for the term. Of course, if the employee chooses to quit, or the employer chooses to fire the employee, the law will not compel fulfillment of the contract.

The second item to specify is the wage. Unless you are a large employer (i.e., with 45 or more employees), or are engaged in interstate commerce (i.e., with gross sales of $500,000 or more), you will not have to comply with federal minimum-wage laws (although most states have their own minimum-wage laws). Beyond the requirements imposed by this law, the amount of remuneration is open to bargaining.

If the contract does not specify a salary, the law will presume a reasonable wage for the work performed. If you hire a salesperson, and the accepted salary in your region for a qualified salesperson is $10 per hour, then it will be presumed that the salesperson was hired for this amount unless you and that person have agreed to a different salary. Thus you cannot escape paying your employees fairly by not discussing the amount they will earn.

In addition to an hourly wage or monthly salary, there are other benefits that you may wish to offer an employee, such as health and life insurance or retirement pensions. Some legal advice may be necessary here in order to take advantage of tax laws.

Third, it is often wise to spell out your employee's duties in the employment contract. This serves as a form of orientation for the employee and also may limit future conflicts over what is and what is not involved in the job.

Fourth, you may want your employee to agree not to work for someone else while working for you or, more important, not to compete with you at the end of the employment period. The latter terms must be carefully drawn to be enforceable. The agreement must be quite specific as to the kind of work the employee may not do; the restriction must apply within a geographic area no broader than that in which you actually operate; and it must apply for a reasonable duration (a five-year period has been upheld). Some states consider these types of agreements as being against their public policies; others enforce them only if they are entered into when the employee is first hired.

The contract should also address the confidentiality of trade secrets—things such as customer lists, supplier lists, and unique sales techniques. "Trade secret" is defined in the Uniform Trade Secret Act as anything that provides its owner with a commercial advantage. Anyone who obtains a trade secret through improper means and exploits it may be prohibited from continuing to use it and may be liable for any provable damages caused to the prior employee. For this reason, your employment contract should specify that if the employee has been exposed to anyone else's trade secrets, he or she will not use them while working for you.

The employee should also acknowledge in the employment contract receipt, in confidence, of your trade secrets and should agree not to use or reveal them without your prior written permission. It is customary to require employees who resign or are terminated to return to the employer all materials containing any of the employer's trade secrets. You should conduct "exit interviews" to remind employees not to use or disclose your trade secrets after leaving your employ.

Finally, the employment contract should specify the grounds for termination of the contract. Even if the contract is terminable at will, these grounds serve as useful guidelines for your employee.

You are vicariously liable for the negligence and, sometimes, even the intentional wrongdoing of your employee when the employee is acting on your behalf. For example, if your employee is at fault in an automobile accident while on the job, you and your employee are both legally liable. So, it's wise to be extremely careful when hiring, and to contact your insurance agent to obtain sufficient insurance coverage for your additional exposure.

Financial and Legal Considerations

When hiring an employee, there are also local, state, and federal laws to consider. The requirements of these laws may vary dramatically, so consult with your lawyer, accountant, and bookkeeper when considering the following:

1. A workers' compensation insurance policy for your employees in the event of on-the-job injury or occupational illness. State laws vary as to how many employees you can have before you are required to offer workers' compensation. The laws in most states provide that an employer who has failed to obtain or keep in force required workers' compensation insurance will be strictly liable, even in the absence of negligence, for on-the-job injury or illness, including not only medical expenses, but also damages for pain and suffering, lost earning potential, and other damages that are a consequence of injuries.

2. Withholding taxes—federal, state, and local. Here, too, the laws vary, so find out what is required in your locale.

3. Social Security (FICA). There are some exemptions. Contact your nearby Social Security office to determine how they may affect you.

4. Unemployment insurance—federal and state. These also include certain technical requirements for subcontractors, etc. You should check with your accountant or attorney to determine what these are.

5. Health and safety regulations—federal and state.

6. Municipal taxes for specific programs, such as schools or public transportation.

7. Employee benefits, such as insurance coverage (medical, dental, legal), retirement benefits, memberships, parking, etc.

8. Union requirements, if you or your employees are subject to union contracts.

9. Wage and hour laws—both federal and state. These include minimum-wage and overtime

requirements. In some states the law also regulates holidays and vacations, as well as the method of paying employees during employment and upon termination.

10. Other forms of employment legislation, such as licensing requirements, that may apply to you, your employees, or your business.

Hazards in the Workplace

Research the potentially toxic effects of all substances used in the art or crafts you sell, whether they are labeled for toxicity or not. You should then disclose to your employees at the time of hiring any pertinent information regarding hazardous substances.

Congress and federal administrative agencies are becoming more active in regulating hazardous substances. You should also be aware that your state workers' compensation agency or the Occupational Safety and Health Administration may have passed special rules regarding specific workplace substances and activities. It is critical to obtain a lawyer's opinion as to whether any of these regulations apply to your gallery or shop. Your state's labor department may also be able to give you information regarding applicable workplace regulations.

Many manufacturers of art and craft supplies voluntarily have begun to label their materials with health and safety warnings. Several states, including California and Oregon, have enacted state art and craft labeling laws. Advocates of a healthy workplace are actively lobbying for similar laws throughout the United States. In response to pressure from these groups, the U.S. Congress in 1979 considered a federal law entitled the Federal Art Hazard Bill. After shuttling through several committees, it died in 1981, but a version of it was finally enacted in 1988, and became effective in 1990. The implementing regulations are still being finalized.

Your lawyer may not be able to tell you exactly to what extent you are legally obligated to advise your employees of the potential risks inherent in their jobs. The best course is to advise the newly hired individual of all known hazards that may result from the work and to disclose the fact that there may be other undiscovered risks in handling the art or craft work. If you have an employment contract, include a paragraph containing such a disclosure and a statement of the employee's acknowledgment of the known risks. Include a similar statement in the employee handbook, if you have one.

While these documents would not provide a defense to a worker's compensation claim, they would sensitize employees to the need for caution in working with the toxic materials. Needless to say, you should take all precautions possible to protect the health and safety of your employees.

Discrimination

Art gallery owners and craft retailers should be aware of the numerous state and federal prohibitions against discrimination on the basis of race, religion, creed, national origin, sex, age, and disability. You should not only be aware of your employees' rights, but also those of your customers and suppliers. The law in this area is constantly changing and you should have an experienced labor attorney assist you in establishing acceptable policies. He or she should should review your advertisements for job applicants and application forms. Your employee handbooks should have a section dealing with prohibitions against discrimination, and guidelines for dealing with customers, suppliers, and any other individuals encountered in the course of doing business.

Although an in-depth analysis of the various federal, state, and local antidiscrimination laws is beyond the scope of this book, a good rule of thumb is to treat everyone with the same respect and dignity you expect to be treated with yourself.

Termination of Employees

As I already mentioned, if the individual working for you is an independent contractor, the contract between you and that person will govern your respective rights of termination. If the individual is an employee, however, you must take care to avoid a wrongful termination when dismissing the individual. The liability for wrongful termination can be catastrophic to a small business.

Historically, an employee who was not under contract could be terminated for any reason whatsoever. More than 25 years ago, this right of absolute dismissal was challenged, and the rule was modified. At that time, it was held that an employee could be terminated for the right reason or for no reason at all, but could not be terminated for the wrong reason. So, for example, an employee who was terminated for refusing to commit perjury before a legislative committee was entitled to recover against the employer for wrongful termination.

Courts have become even more protective of the rights of employees. In a 1983 case, *Novosel v. Nationwide Insurance Company*, the United States Circuit Court of Appeals held that the power to hire and fire could not be used to dictate an employee's political activity. The court, in essence, held that one's right to exercise constitutionally protected free speech was more important than the employer's right to control an employee's conduct.

In an Arizona case, the state Supreme Court held that an employee who was terminated for refusing to "moon" fellow employees in a parody of the song "Moon River" during a company retreat was entitled to damage for wrongful termination. The public policy of protecting her right of privacy was deemed more important than the employer's right to terminate employees for disobedience.

Employers may not legally fire someone for any one of these three reasons:

1. For refusing to commit an unlawful act, such as committing perjury or refusing to participate in illegal price-fixing schemes

2. For performing a public obligation, such as serving on a jury or serving in a military reserve unit

3. For exercising a statutory right, such as filing a claim for workers' compensation

A number of states have considered adopting legislation that would restrict the employer's right to terminate an employee to those cases in which there was just cause. These laws also contain specific prohibitions on the termination of employees for "whistle-blowing", that is, notifying government authorities of wrongful acts by the employer, such as tax evasion, or notifying corporate officers of wrongful acts of the employee's immediate supervisors.

An employer should have a legend in the employee handbook that makes it clear that the handbook is not an employment contract. Oral statements by recruiters or interviewers might also be construed as imposing obligations on the employer. Employers often require prospective employees to sign a statement making it clear that the employment is at will and does not give rise to any contractual rights. If there is a probationary period after the hire, the employer should be careful to state that after the probationary period, the employee will become a regular or full-time employee, not a permanent employee.

In addition, any evaluation of the employee after the probationary period should be conducted fairly. When evaluations become merely pro forma, problems can and do arise. Employees may argue that they have received sparkling evaluations and are being terminated for an invalid reason.

To avoid misunderstanding or dispute, the employer should use what has been characterized as progressive discipline. The procedure begins with a verbal warning to an employee of your concern about a performance problem. If the problem persists, disciplinary practices are taken progressively until termination is the only form of recourse left. The entire process should be documented in the employee file.

When in doubt, an employer should contact an attorney with some experience in the field of employment relations. In this area, as with many others, preproblem counseling can prevent a good deal of time consuming and costly litigation.

CHAPTER 11
Pension Plans as Employee Benefits

■ ONE OF THE METHODS by which a gallery owner may attract and retain key personnel is to provide certain benefits. Today one of the most important benefits for employees is the ability to participate in a pension plan.

A pension plan is a written savings program. If the plan meets the IRS's specific rules and regulations, it is a so called "qualified" plan and then contributions are tax deductible to the person or the business making the investments. The earnings will grow, free of all taxes either to the plan sponsor or the participants.

A qualified plan is the last remaining tax shelter available to highly compensated individuals. It may be used to set aside funds for retirement, and to attract and retain key employees. If properly structured and funded on a conservative basis with diversified portfolio investments, the plan should achieve financial security for the individual's retirement.

When choosing a plan, select the type that will most satisfactorily meet your needs and those of your employees. There are two types of qualified plans: defined contribution and defined benefit plans.

Defined Contribution Plans

In a defined contribution plan, the contributions to the plan are defined—that is, the amount of money that is invested on behalf of the participant is "defined" as a percentage of the participant's annual income. The amount of money that will be available to the participant at retirement is not defined. Interest and earnings on the invest-

ments made through the plan increase the retirement benefit for the individual plan participants. The longer the period of time over which investments are accumulated and interest is earned, the greater the amount of benefits that will be available to the participant at retirement.

Profit-sharing plans, salary savings or reduction plans (such as 401K), and money purchase plans are all defined contribution plans, as are Simplified Employee Pension Plans (SEPPs) and Employee Stock Ownership Plans (ESOPs).

Profit-Sharing Plans

If the revenue (income) from your business varies significantly from year to year, a profit-sharing plan may be the most appropriate type of plan to offer to your employees. Contributions are determined at the end of the accounting year, which is usually December 31. Contributions to the plan can be determined annually by a vote of your business's management (i.e., managing partners or the board of directors), or by a formula previously designated in the plan's documents. Recent changes in federal laws no longer require a corporation to declare a profit in order to make a contribution. Contributions to a profit-sharing plan are limited to a maximum of 15 percent of an employee's annual income and cannot exceed total contributions of $30,000 per year for each participant.

Salary Savings/Reduction Plans (also known as Thrift Plans)

These plans, which include 401Ks, are a variant of profit-sharing plans. Under this type of plan, the employee elects to have a percentage of his or her gross salary diverted into a qualified plan. The employee's contributions are pretax dollars, so this type of plan provides the employee with a significant tax savings. Depending on the plan, the employer may elect to match a portion of the contributions made by the employee. Usually the amount of the matching contribution has a limit.

The main feature of salary savings/reduction plans is that a portion of the cost shifts from the employer to the employee; the business therefore makes less of a cash contribution to this type of pension plan.

A major drawback is the limitation of contributions by highly compensated employees. In 1991, for example, the maximum amount of an employee's contribution was limited to approximately $8,475; for 1992, the maximum contribution was $8,994. In addition, total contributions to the plan on behalf of the top one-third of highly compensated employees are dictated by the lower two-thirds of compensated employees, because employees must contribute the indentical percentage of their income. If, therefore, the less highly compensated employees wish to contribute three percent of their income, the highly compensated employees may only contribute three percent of their income up to the statutory limit. Although there are exceptions, generally this plan is appropriate only in companies with at least 25 employees.

Simplified Employee Pension Plans (SEPPs)

These plans are often viewed incorrectly as an alternative to the more highly structured qualified plans. The maximum contribution is $30,000 per annum. Contributions are based on an equal percentage of annual salary for all employees 21 years or older, who have performed service for the employer during at least three out of five years and have received at least $363. Although its low maintenance cost is an initial attraction, its simplicity results in a significant inflexibility that many employers are not willing to accept.

Money Purchase Plans

Under this type of plan, the employer determines how much he or she wants to save each year. Although there are other restrictions, the primary parameters are: the lesser of 25 percent of annual income (20 percent of the gross earnings for the unincorporated gallery owner or retailer), or $30,000 in contributions per year per participant.

Employee Stock Ownership Plans (ESOPs)

In each of the defined contribution plans already discussed, the employer is specifically prohibited from owning more than ten percent of the stock in the parent sponsor corporation as an asset of the plan.

In an ESOP plan, the majority of the assets are shares of stock in the parent corporation. Generally, ESOPs are not useful for owners of small businesses.

Defined Benefit Plans

Contributions to a defined benefit plan are determined by a relatively complex formula, and then monitored by a professionally licensed enrolled actuary. Contributions to a defined benefit plan are not to exceed the lesser of 100 percent of the employee's annual average income for the three highest-salaried consecutive years or a specified amount, which is adjusted annually and dependent on changes in the Consumer Price Index. (For 1991, the maximum amount of contributions to a defined benefit plan was $108,963 per year; for 1992, it was $115,641.)

Excess earnings (investment income) greater than the assumptions made by the actuary (normally eight percent) are used to reduce the cost of contributions to the plan by the employer.

Normally, defined benefit plans are appropriate where the gallery owner or crafts retailer is "mature", with less than 10-15 working years until retirement.

Defined benefit plans are appropriate—and potentially beneficial—for businesses that have enjoyed considerable financial success with limited fluctuations in cash flow. The defined benefit plan can be designed to drain excess funds and allocate them to retirement on behalf of the senior preferred participant (the principal owner). In many instances, this same advantage can be attained through the use of a target benefit plan.

Target Benefit Plans

The target benefit plan is receiving renewed interest, as a result of changes in income-tax law. This hybrid plan combines the contribution and benefit levels of a defined contribution plan with the recognition for senior (older) employees found in defined benefit plans.

As a result of changes under the Technical Corrections Act of 1987, a second addition to this hybrid category, known as an Age-Weighted Profit-Sharing Plan (AWPSP), has been developed. As with the target benefit plan, the contributions to this profit-sharing plan are "weighted" or skewed toward senior employees.

Designing and Documenting a Plan

The creation of a qualified plan usually involves the creation and adoption of a trust agreement, disclosure of information for employees, and other pertinent language. As I mentioned earlier, plans must be in writing. Plans containing the standardized language preapproved by the IRS are available from several sources, including insurance companies, brokerage houses, and mutual fund companies. Each of these sources may have limitations, either in the language, investment opportunities, or requirements for the use of a third-party trustee that should be carefully evaluated. It is, therefore, essential to work with an experienced professional when selecting and establishing a plan.

Since 1982, Federal Tax Laws have been amended to allow unincorporated businesses the same status as corporations with regard to qualified pension plans. Further, this same legislation eliminated the need for a third-party administrator, thus allowing the employer to be the trustee (that is, the caretaker) of his or her own plan.

Plans may be combined or "stacked" to more specifically meet the needs of the business; however, this creates the need for separate sets of rules and limitations. Stacking also increases the amount of administrative paperwork and forms, thus driving up the cost of operating and maintaining the plan.

The design features outlined below can be used to limit or reduce the cost or participation by employees in the employer-sponsored plan.

Testing

A key element of any qualified plan is to reward long-term service by employees. One method used to limit participation by employees who have been employed for a relatively short period of time is a vesting schedule. Currently, for small plans, the IRS recognizes two primary vesting formulas:

1. Five-year exclusion with 100 percent vesting (also known as "cliff" vesting, because it is all or nothing, like falling off a cliff). This formula does not allow vesting for employees with less than five years of service. Upon completion of five years of service, the employee is 100 percent vested in the plan.

2. Three- to seven-year graded vesting. This vesting formula can preclude participation by an employee until the employee has worked for at least one plan year. Following completion of the third plan year of employment, for the subsequent 12 months, the employee would be entitled to 20 percent of the funds that have been set aside for him or her. For each subsequent year of participation in the plan, the employee is vested an additional 20 percent. After completing seven years of plan participation, the employee is eligible to receive 100

percent of the contributions and interest earnings on the funds upon termination of employment.

Minimum Hours

The plan sponsor may limit the participation of employees by exempting those who work fewer than 500 hours per year. This feature is very important for businesses that retain temporary employees.

Minimum Age

The plan sponsor may also limit participation of employees through the use of a minimum age requirement. Current law allows an employer to postpone participation by employees under 21 years of age. At the time the employee reaches age 21, his or her total years of service must be applied to the vesting formula.

Integration

This feature allows the plan sponsor to recognize contributions made on behalf of the employee to Social Security. The plan sponsor applies two separate levels of contribution. The first is a minimum contribution up to the maximum contributions under Social Security. The second is on all income in excess of the first level. Current tax statutes limit the separation of the two levels of contributions to seven percent.

Union

Employees that are a part of a collective bargaining unit can be specifically exempted from participation in a qualified plan established by an employer.

Investments in a Qualified Plan

The primary governing factor regarding investments made by a qualified plan is contained in the Internal Revenue Code (IRC) statement known as "The Prudent Person Investment Principle." This means that investments should be made with primary consideration given to the preservation of salary or principal (amounts invested), and secondary consideration to growth and income.

Growth

In an investment, growth occurs when the original principal or amount invested increases in value—for example, shares of stocked purchased at $1 per share increase in value to $1.25 per share.

Income

Income is derived through a principal investment that earns interest. Two of the most frequent questions asked are: "What investments should I use in my pension plan? and how much should I invest in each one?"

There is a plethora of investment opportunities, including stocks, bonds, money market accounts, real estate, partnership interests, etc. Therefore, it is essential that you confer with a qualified financial planner to structure your plan investments based on your goals, the economy, and other relevant factors.

CHAPTER 12
Copyright

■ ART GALLERIES AND CRAFT retailers must be sensitive to the complex legal rules surrounding copyright. These rules pertain not only to the art or craft works you market, but also to the advertising, catalogs, flyers, and posters you may use in your business.

Copyright law in the United States has its foundations in the Constitution, which provides that Congress shall have the power "to promote the progress of science and the useful arts, by securing for limited time to authors and inventors the exclusive right to their respective writings and discoveries." The first Congress enacted a copyright law, revised by later Congresses.

When the Copyright Act of 1909 was passed, the printing press was still the primary means of disseminating information. One of the problems with the 1909 Act was that it was not the exclusive source of copyright law. Copyright protection or its equivalent was also provided by common law (that body of law developed by the courts independent of statutes) and various state laws, and this caused considerable confusion. Also, new technology, such as improved printing processes, radio, television, videotape, computer software, and microfilm, created the need for a revision.

The Copyright Revision Act of 1976 became effective on January 1, 1978, and is the only legislation that covers works created or published on or after that date. The creation of copyright in all works published prior to January 1, 1978, is governed by the 1909 Act. For these works, however, rights other than creation, such as duration of copyright, infringement penalties, and infringement remedies are governed by the new law.

What Is Copyright?

A copyright is actually a granting of five exclusive rights. First is the right to reproduce a work by any means. The scope of this right can be hard to define, especially when it involves photocopying, microform, videotape, the creation of functional arts, etc. (Under the Copyright Act of 1976, someone may reproduce protected works without permission if such reproduction involves fair use or an exempted use, which I'll explain later in this chapter.) The copyright law makes it clear that customers should not be permitted the right to photograph work in a gallery or shop. You may request slides and photos from the artists to keep in your files and archives, but these works can only be used in promotional material and only if you obtained permission from the artist to do so. This permission, if provable, is enforceable.

Second is the right to prepare derivative works based on the copyrighted work. A derivative work is one that transforms or adapts the subject matter of one or more preexisting works—for example, a poster bearing the image of a piece of sculpture or a fiber piece containing designs that are in the public domain.

Third is the right to distribute copies to the public for sale or lease. Once a person sells a copyrighted work or permits uncontrolled distribution, however, the right to control the further use of that work usually ends. This is known as the "first sale" doctrine, and does not apply if the work is merely in the possession of someone else temporarily—as in a rental or lease—or if the copyright owner has a contract with the purchaser restricting the purchaser's freedom to use the work.

It's important to understand the distinction between the sale of a work and the sale of the copyright in that work. If nothing is said about copyright when the work is sold, the artist retains the copyright. Your customers may not be aware of this, so you may wish to call it to their attention in the bill of sale. If a license of rights covered by copyright is granted, the scope of the rights being granted should be specified in writing. For example, if a collector is granted the right to photograph a painting for Christmas cards, can the image also be used to make posters? The answer is "no", unless the drafter of the license has specified that as a permissible use.

Fourth is the right to perform a work publicly, for example, to broadcast a film or promotional video received from an artist on television or to show it in a lecture room or meeting room.

Fifth is the right to display the work publicly. Once the copyright owner has sold a copy of the work, the purchaser has the right to display that copy but generally does not have permission to reproduce it.

Who Owns the Copyright?

As a general rule, the creator of a work owns the copyright. Under the 1909 law, which still applies to works created before January 1, 1978, when a work is sold, ownership of a common-law copyright passed to the purchaser unless the creator reserved the copyright in a written agreement. Under the Copyright Act of 1976, unless there is a written agreement to the contrary, the creator retains the copyright when the work is sold.

Creators of a joint work are co-owners of the copyright in the work. A joint work is a work prepared by more than one person "with the intention that their contributions be merged into inseparable or interdependent parts of a unitary whole." Whatever profit one creator makes from use of the work must be shared equally with the others unless they have a written agreement that states otherwise. If there is no intention to create a single, indivisible work, each creator may own the copyright to his or her individual contribution. For example, if two sculptors arrange to have each of their unique creations complement and fit next to the other's work, then each would own the rights only to his or her own individual work.

Works for Hire

Works considered to be "works for hire" are an important exception to the general rule that a person owns the copyright in a work he or she has created. If a work was created by an employee on the job, the law considers the product a work for hire, and the employer owns the copyright, unless there is a written contract that clearly states that the copyrightable material in question is not part of the "scope of employment".

In *Peregrine v. Lauren Corp.*, the court found that a photographer's work was work for hire because the advertising agency that employed him had the right to supervise and control the photographer's work. Courts also consider the amount of an employer's artistic advice before, during, and after the work was created to determine whether a creator is working for hire as opposed to working as an independent contractor (see p. 48).

Unless there is a contractual agreement to the contrary, the independent contractor owns the copyright. If the creator is an independent contractor, the works will be considered works for hire only if (1) the parties have signed a written agreement to that effect, and (2) the work is specially ordered or commissioned as a contribution to a collective work, a supplementary work (one that introduces, revises, comments upon, or assists a work by another), a compilation, a translation, an instructional text, answer material for a test, an atlas, a motion picture, or an audiovisual work.

Transferring or Licensing Copyright

A copyright owner may sell the entire copyright or any part of it, or may license any right within it. The rights must be specifically identified and transferred through a written contract, which must then be signed by the copyright owner or the owner's authorized agent. The licensing contract must state the scope, duration, frequency of use, type of use, etc. A license authorizing a particular use of a work can be granted orally, but is revocable at the will of the copyright owner.

Often an art gallery owner or crafts retailer will become the assignee of ownership or licensee of the creator's copyright. This allows the dealer to incorporate the artist's or craftsperson's copyrighted work into the dealer's work—for example, to include photographs of art or crafts in a catalog.

Both an assignment of ownership of copyright and a licensing agreement should be recorded with the Copyright Office. The cost to record a transfer is only $20 and is a tax-deductible business expense. When the transaction is recorded, the rights of the assignee or licensee are protected in much the same way as the rights of an owner of real estate are protected by recording the deed. In a case of conflicting transfers of rights, if both transactions are recorded within one month of the execution, the person whose transaction was completed first prevails. If the transactions are not recorded within a month of the execution, the one who records first prevails. A nonexclusive license prevails over any unrecorded transfer of ownership. Before an assignee or a licensee can sue a third party for infringement, the document of transfer must be recorded.

Termination of Copyright Transfers and Licenses

It is not unusual for a copyright owner to transfer all rights in the copyright for a pittance, only to see the work become valuable at a later date. The 1976 Copyright Act offers a remedy for this injustice. It provides that, after a certain period has lapsed, the creator of the original work or certain other parties may terminate the transfer of the copyright and reclaim the rights. The creator

then has a second chance to market and benefit from his or her work. This right to terminate a transfer is called a "termination interest".

In most cases, the termination interest belongs to the creator. But if the creator is deceased and is survived by a spouse but no children, the surviving spouse owns the termination interest. If the deceased creator is not survived by a spouse, ownership of the interest belongs to any surviving children in equal shares. If the decedent is survived by both spouse and children, the interest is divided so that the spouse receives fifty percent and the children receive equal shares of the remaining fifty percent.

If the termination interest is owned by more than one party, a majority of the owners must agree to terminate the transfer. Under the 1976 Act, the general rule is that termination may be effected at any time within a five-year period beginning at the end of the 35th year from the date the rights were transferred. If, however, the transfer included the right of publication, termination may go into effect at any time within a five-year period, beginning at the end of 35 years from the date of publication, or 40 years from the date of transfer, whichever occurred first.

The party wishing to terminate the transferred interest must serve an advance written notice on the transferee. This notice must state the intended termination date and must be served not less than two and no more than ten years prior to the stated termination date. A copy of the notice must be recorded in the Copyright Office before the effective date of termination.

What Can Be Copyrighted?

An author, from the point of view of copyright law, is a creator—whether photographer, sculptor, writer, or craftsperson. Congress grants copyright protection to "original works of authorship fixed in any tangible medium of expression." (In 1980 the Act was amended to include computer software.) Originality—as distinguished from uniqueness—requires that a work be created independently, but does not require that it be the only one of its kind. In the past, the Copyright Office occasionally denied protection to works it considered immoral or obscene, even though it had no express authority to do so. Today, copyright registration is not refused because of the content of the work.

The 1976 Act expressly exempts from copyright protection "any idea, procedure, process, system, method of operation, concept, principle, or discovery." In short, a copyright extends only to the "expression" of creations of the mind, not to the ideas themselves. Frequently, there is no clear line of division between an idea and its expression, but a pure idea, such as a concept for a work of art, as distinguished from the tangible art itself, cannot be copyrighted, no matter how original or creative it is.

Not everything in a copyrighted work is protected. For example, the title of a work cannot be copyrighted. Rather, it may be protected under the trademark laws (see Chapter 13). A related issue is whether functional art, such as rugs, clothing, and the like, is copyrightable. If the aesthetics of the work can exist separately from and be identified independently of the functional, then the aesthetic portion of the work is copyrightable. For example, the creator of slippers in the shape of animal feet was granted a copyright in the artistic portion of the functional item. Potters have obtained copyrights for the surface designs of their pottery, although not for the pottery itself.

Public Domain

Once the copyright on a work has expired, or has been lost through failure to comply with the notice requirement prior to March 1, 1989, the effective date of the Bern Treaty, the work enters the public domain, where it can be used by anyone in any manner. A person can, however, obtain copyright on a work derived from a work in the public domain if a distinguishable variation is created. This means, for example, that Rembrandt's painting "Night Watch" cannot be copyrighted, but a photograph of it can. As a result, no one

would be able to copy the photograph, whereas anyone would be able to copy Rembrandt's original. The photograph is a copyrightable derivative work of a preexisting work.

Other examples of copyrightable derivative works include collages, photographs of photographs, film versions, and any other work "recast, transformed, or adapted" from the original. You must, however, when registering the derivative work, disclose that it is based on a work in the public domain.

Compilations

Compilations are also copyrightable, as long as the preexisting materials are gathered and arranged in a new or original form. Compilations such as catalogs, magazines, pamphlets, or books can be copyrightable as a whole even though individual contributions are individually copyrighted. The underlying facts or ideas upon which the compilation is based may not be protected, however, if they do not satisfy the creativity requirement. For example, in *Feist Publications, Inc. v. Rural Telephone Service Company, Inc,.* the U.S. Supreme Court held that a phone book was not copyrightable because the alphabetical arrangement was not creative.

Publication

In copyright law, the concept of publication is different from what a lay person might expect it to be. "Publication," according to the 1976 Act, is "the distribution of copies of a work to the public by sale or other transfer of ownership, or by rental, lease, or loan."

A public performance or display of a work does not of itself constitute publication. Under the Copyright Act of 1909, when a person showed copies of a work to close friends or associates with the understanding that such copies were not to be further reproduced and distributed, the person had not published the work. A distribution of works to agents or customers for purposes of review and criticism also does not constitute a publication.

Under this doctrine of limited publication, publication does not occur when a person displays work "to a definitely selected group and for a limited purpose, without the right of diffusion, reproduction, distribution, or sale."

The Copyright Revision Act of 1976 makes no specific reference to this doctrine of limited publication, but the statutory definition of publication requires a "distribution of copies or phonorecords of a work to the public." A congressional report explains that "the public" in this context refers to people who are under no explicit or implicit restrictions with respect to disclosure of the work's contents. It is, therfore, believed that the limited publication doctrine is continued under the new law.

Duration of Copyright

The Constitution permits Congress to grant copyright protection only "for limited times." Under the 1976 Act, copyright exists throughout the life of the creator plus 50 years. If the work is created jointly, the copyright expires 50 years after the last author dies. (The Copyright Office keeps records of famous authors' deaths as of the mid-1960s, but if the office does not have a record of a author's death, they assume the author or authors are dead 75 years after the first publication date or 100 years after creation, whichever occurs first. This applies equally to composite works, anonymous, and pseudonymous works.)

Under the 1976 Act, there are no renewals for copyrights on works created on or after January 1, 1978. The 1909 Copyright Act, however, granted a creator copyright protection for a 28-year period, which could then be renewed for one additional 28-year period. Under the 1976 Act, copyrights granted under the 1909 Act and still in their first 28-year term as of January 1, 1978, will continue for the remainder of the 28-year term and will automatically be renewed for another 47

years, for a total of 75 years. Copyrights granted under the 1909 Act and in their second 28-year term as of January 1, 1978, automatically received an extension duration to create a term of 75 years from the date copyright was first obtained. In all cases, copyright terms end on December 31 of the given year.

Unpublished works that were fixed in a tangible medium prior to January 1, 1978, are in a special category with regard to the duration of copyright protection. Because they are unpublished, they are not covered by the 1909 Act. Because they were fixed in a tangible medium prior to January 1, 1978, they are not covered by the 1976 Act. Prior to the 1976 Act, these types of works were covered by common law, which protected them in perpetuity, but the 1976 Act extends federal protection for these works for the author's life plus 50 years.

The earliest date when such a copyright can expire is December 31, 2002. If the creator or owner of unpublished works publishes before that date, the term of copyright shall not expire before December 31, 2027, a 25-year extension.

Creation of Copyright

As I mentioned earlier, all copyrightable works are automatically protected by the federal copyright law as soon as they are fixed in a tangible medium, without the formal requirements of registration or deposit of copies.

Unpublished works can be registered with the Copyright Office, and must be registered before an infringement suit can be filed. Care should be taken to disclose all material facts about the work in the registration. A prepublication registration can be made after the infringement, as long as the registration occurs before filing the suit. One of the advantages to early registration is that after five years the facts contained in the registration are presumed to be true. In the event of an infringement suit, this presumption, which will hold even after the work is published, can greatly simplify the copyright owner's preparation for trial and recovery of court costs and attorney's fees.

Copyright Notice

Copyright notice should be used to avoid someone's copying the work in the belief that it is in the public domain. Even though the 1976 Act allows the author copyright on works published without notice, and the 1989 revision does not require notice, a person who copies a work believing it is in the public domain because there is no notice is considered an innocent infringer. In this situation, the author whose work was copied cannot recover damages; in fact, a court might allow the copier to continue using the work. The 1989 amendment provides that if the notice is used, an infringer cannot claim that the infringement was innocent.

A copyright notice has three elements, as required by the Universal Copyright Convention (UCC). First is the word "copyright" (or any understandable abbreviation) or the international copyright symbol ©. No variation in the symbol is permitted. For example, the Copyright Office determined that the use of "(c)" in copyright notices in computer programs did not satisfy the notice requirement.

The second element is the year of first publication (or, in the case of unpublished works governed by the 1909 Act, the year in which the copyright was registered). The duration of the copyright of a work or a work for hire is measured from the date either of creation or of first publication. This date may be expressed in Arabic or Roman numerals or in words.

A derivative (or revised) work covered by the 1909 Act would have had to carry both the date of the original work and that of the revision. Under the 1976 Act, the date of the first publication of the revised work is sufficient. The 1976 Act allows the year to be omitted in some very specific cases, but because the date is necessary for some international protection, it should always be included.

The third element of a copyright notice is the name of the copyright owner. If there are several owners, one name is sufficient. Usually the author's full name is used, but if the author is well known by a last name, the last name can be used alone or with initials. A business that owns a copyright may use its trade name if the name is legally recognized in its state.

Copyright notice for a photograph by the author of this book could be presented in one of three ways:

Copr. 1991 Leonard D. DuBoff

or

© 1991 Leonard D. DuBoff

or

Copyright 1991 Leonard D. DuBoff

If international protection is desired, the copyright owner may have to supply additional text to the copyright notice. Under the Buenos Aires Convention (which includes most Central and South American countries as well as the United States), the statement "all rights reserved", in either Spanish or English, must be included in the notice. If there is any possibility that the work will be sold in Central or South America, include this statement.

If these three elements of copyright notice are present, the work will be protected in any UCC signatory country in which it is sold, in the same way in which that country protects its own nationals. The United States and most European nations have signed the UCC, but UCC protection is available only for American works first published in the United States after the convention became effective, on September 16, 1955. Thus, works first published in the United States before that date are not entitled to UCC protection. Nevertheless, such works are entitled to international protection under the Bern Convention, if the works were simultaneously published in the United States and a Bern signatory country.

The United States became a party to the Bern Convention on October 31, 1988. Therefore, publication in the United States now gives Bern protection without publication in another Bern signatory nation. The Bern Convention prohibits a signatory nation from requiring that a copyright notice be placed on a work as a condition for copyright protection. The U.S. Copyright Law was therefore amended effective March 1, 1989, to permit protection without notice. Notice is still required, however, for other treaty protection and to prevent innocent infringement.

Errors in or Omission of a Copyright Notice

Under the 1909 Act, with few exceptions, any omission, misplacement, or imperfection in the notice on any copy of a work distributed by authority of the copyright owner placed the work forever in the public domain. The copyright was lost if the wrong name appeared in the notice. If the sale of copyright was not recorded with the Copyright Office, use of the new owner's name in the notice invalidated the copyright. If an earlier date was used, the copyright term would be measured from that year, thereby decreasing the duration of protection. If a later date was used, the copyright was forfeited and the work entered the public domain (although a mistake of one year was not penalized). Publishers went to great lengths to protect the printing plates containing the copyright notice, because if one letter or number in the notice was accidentally chipped or broken, the copyright notice might be invalid.

The notice requirements are not as stringent for works published between January 1, 1978, and March 1, 1989, and notice is not required at all after March 1, 1989. Although the 1976 Act gives the Copyright Office the authority to regulate where the copyright should be placed, failure to comply with these regulations is not automatically fatal to the copyright. A mistake in the name is also not fatal, however an infringer who is honestly misled by the incorrect name can use this as a defense to a suit for copyright infringement if the proper name was not registered with the Copyright Office.

Under the 1976 Act, the use of a later date will not be of any consequence when the duration of the copyright is determined by the author's life.

When the duration of the copyright is determined by the date of first publication, as in the case of a composite work, work for hire, or work copyrighted by a corporation, the later date will be used to measure how long the copyright will last. If an earlier year is used, the work is considered to have been published without notice.

If a work has been published or republished without notice between January 1, 1978 and March 1, 1989, the copyright owner is still protected for five years. If during those five years the owner registers the copyright with the Copyright Office and makes a reasonable effort to place a notice on copies of the works that were published without notice and distributed within the United States, full copyright protection would be granted for the appropriate duration of the published work. To place a notice on copies that have been sold, notification of the oversight should be sent to agencies, stores, or owners that distribute or sell the work. Adhesive stickers, displaying the correct copyright notice, should be sent with a request that they be attached to the works. If the notice was omitted only from a relatively small number of copies, the owner need not register at all. The risk of loss of copyright, however, is not worth the gamble on how many copies constitute a "relatively small number". If there is any doubt, the author should register and attempt to get the correction notice placed on all copies.

A copyright owner is forgiven for an omission of notice if the error was made by another party who had been licensed the right to publish and had been required to include proper notice. The validity of the copyright is also not effected if the notice is removed or obliterated by an unauthorized person.

If someone infringes copyright as a result of omission of or error in copyright, the person generally would not be penalized. In some cases, however, the innocent infringer may be compelled to surrender any profits made from the infringement. On the other hand, if the infringer made a sizable investment for future production, the court may compel the copyright owner to grant a license to the infringer.

Registration and Deposit

Copyright protection is automatic when an idea is "fixed in a tangible medium of expression," and placement of copyright notice identifies the copyright owner. Neither action, however, constitutes official notice to the U.S. government. In order to officially register copyright, and assure yourself that your work is protected, you need to complete a registration application and send a registration fee and copies of the protected work to the Register of Copyrights.

The 1976 Act specifies that the copyright owner cannot bring a lawsuit to enforce his or her copyright until the copyright has been registered. If the copyright is registered prior to the infringement, the owner may be entitled to more complete remedies, including attorney's fees and statutory damages. If copyright is registered after an infringement occurs, the owner's legal remedies are limited. No remedies will be lost if registration is made within three months of publication, so it's best to register the copyright as soon as possible.

To register copyright, you need to complete Form VA for a work of visual art or Form TX for textual material, such as brochures, catalogs, etc. You can obtain copies of both forms from the Register of Copyrights, Library of Congress, Washington, DC 20559 (See pp. 130 and 134 for samples of each form.) The forms are brief and straightforward; the instructions accompanying them are short and relatively easy to understand.

The owner of the copyright, or the owner of the exclusive right of publication (usually a publisher or advertiser), must deposit two copies of the "best edition" of the work within three months after the work is published. In the case of an unpublished work or a collective work, only one copy need be deposited. (Once a work has been registered as unpublished, it does not need to be registered again when published.) For works of art and editioned prints where the edition size is 300 or less, two photographs of the work fulfill this requirement. This basic deposit requirement also applies to works published abroad when such works are either imported into the United States or become part of an American publication. Copies deposited at the Copyright Office are transferred to the Library of Congress or other federal libraries. A few deposit copies are transferred to university or public libraries.

Send the completed registration form, a check for $20, andthe required number of copies of the work to the Register of Copyrights, Library of Congress, Washington, DC 20559.

If the required copies are not deposited within the requisite three-month period, the Register of Copyrights may demand them. If the copies are not submitted within three months after demand, the person upon whom demand was made may be subject to a fine of up to $250 for each unsubmitted work. In addition, such person or persons may be required to pay the Library of Congress an amount equal to the retail cost of the work, or, if no retail cost has been established, the costs incurred by the library in acquiring the work, provided such costs are reasonable. Finally, a copyright proprietor who willfully and repeatedly refuses to comply with a demand may be liable for an additional fine of $2,500.

When an application has been processed and approved, the Copyright Office returns the form with a registration number. Although it looks quite informal, this is an official document and should be stored in a safe place. If the registration certificate is lost, it can be replaced for a small fee, but the process may be time consuming.

Copyright Infringement and Remedies

A copyright infringement occurs when an unauthorized person exercises any of the five exclusive rights protected by a copyright. The fact that the infringing party did not intend to improperly use protected rights or did not know that the work was protected by copyright is relevant only with respect to the penalty.

All actions for infringement of copyright must be brought in a federal court within three years of the date of the infringement. The copyright owner must prove that the work was copyrighted and registered, that the infringer had access to and used the copyrighted work, and that the infringer copied a "substantial and material" portion of the copyrighted work. In order to demonstrate the extent of the damage caused by the infringement, the copyright owner must also provide evidence that shows how widely the infringing copies were distributed.

The copyright owner must prove that the infringer had access to the protected work, because an independent creation of an identical work is not an infringement. However, infringement can occur even if an entire work was not copied, because any unauthorized copying of a substantial portion of a work constitutes an infringement.

If the expressions of ideas, rather than simply the ideas alone, are found to be similar, the court must decide whether the similarity is substantial and whether the work itself is copyrighted. This is done in two steps. First, the court looks at the more general similarities of the works, such as subject matter, setting, materials used, and the like. For this, there may be expert testimony. The second step involves a subjective judgment of the works' intrinsic similarity: Would a lay observer recognize that the alleged copy had been appropriated from the copyrighted work? No expert testimony is allowed in making this determination.

Hogan v. MacMillan, Inc., a case in the late 1980s, held that the substantial similarity test applies even when the allegedly infringing material is in a different medium. George Balanchine choreographed The Nutcracker ballet, and his estate receives royalties every time the ballet is performed. MacMillan published a book of photographs that included 60 color pictures of scenes from a performance of The Nutcracker. In determining whether this constituted infringement, the Court of Appeals noted that the correct test is whether "the ordinary observer, unless he set out to detect the disparities, would

be disposed to overlook them, and regard their aesthetic appeal as the same." Furthermore, the court noted, "Even a small amount of the original, if it is qualitatively significant, may be sufficient to be an infringement, although the full original could not be recreated from the excerpt."

Even before the trial, the copyright owner may obtain a preliminary court order against an infringer. The copyright owner can petition the court to seize all copies of the alleged infringing work and the negatives or masters used to produce them. To do this, the copyright owner must file a sworn statement that the work is an infringement and provide a substantial bond approved by the court. After the seizure, the alleged infringer may object to the amount or form of the bond.

After the trial, if the work is held to be an infringement, the court can order the destruction of all copies, and enjoin future infringement. In addition, the copyright owner may be awarded damages. The copyright owner may request that the court award actual damages or statutory damages—a choice that can be made any time before the final judgment is recorded.

Actual damages are either the amount of the financial injury sustained by the copyright owner or, as in most cases, the equivalent of the profits made by the infringer. In proving the infringer's profits, the copyright owner need only establish the gross revenues received for the illegal exploitation of the work. The infringer then must prove any deductible expenses.

The amount of statutory damages is decided by the court, within specified limits: no less than $500 and no more than $20,000. The maximum possible recovery is increased to $100,000 if the copyright owner proves that the infringment was willful. The court has the option to award the prevailing party its costs and attorneys' fees. As I've already mentioned, statutory damages and attorneys' fees may not be awarded if the copyright was not registered prior to infringement, provided such infringement occurred more than three months after the work was published.

The U.S. Justice Department can prosecute a copyright infringer. If the prosecutor proves beyond a reasonable doubt that the infringement was committed willfully and for commercial gain, the infringer can be fined and sentenced to jail. There is also a fine for placing a false copyright notice on a work, for removing or obliterating a copyright notice, or for knowingly making a false statement in an application for a copyright. A number of individuals have been imprisoned for large-scale copyright infringements.

Fair Use

Not every copying of a protected work is an infringement. The Copyright Act of 1976 recognizes that copies of a protected work "for purposes such as criticism, comment, news reporting, teaching (including multiple copies for classroom use), scholarship or research" can be considered fair use and therefore not an infringement. This is not, however, a complete list nor is it intended as a definition of fair use. Fair use, in fact, is not defined by the Act. Instead, the Act cites four criteria to be considered in determining whether a particular use is or is not fair:

1. The purpose and character of the use, including whether it is for commercial use or for nonprofit educational purposes

2. The nature of the copyrighted work

3. The amount and substantiality of the portion used in relation to the copyrighted work as a whole

4. The effect of the use upon the potential market for, or value of, the copyrighted work

The Act does not rank these four criteria, nor does it exclude other factors in determining the question of fair use. In effect, all that the Act does is leave the doctrine of fair use to be developed by the courts.

Photocopying

The limits of fair use are hotly debated in the area of photocopying. The Copyright Act provides that "reproduction in copies . . . for purposes such as criticism, comment, news reporting, teaching (including multiple copies for classroom use), scholarship, or research" can be a fair use. This, however, raises many questions. Reproduction of what? A piece of an image? More than half an image? An image no longer generally available? How many copies? To help answer these questions, several interested organizations drafted a set of guidelines for classroom copying in nonprofit educational institutions. These guidelines are not a part of the Copyright Act, but are printed in the Act's legislative history. Even though the writers of the guidelines defined the guide as "minimum standards of educational fair use", major educational groups have publicly expressed the fear that publishers would attempt to establish the guidelines as maximum standards beyond which there could be no fair use.

As all this demonstrates, it is not easy to define what sorts of uses are fair uses. Questions continue to be resolved on a case-by-case basis. You should consult a lawyer when it appears that one of your works has been infringed or when you intend to use someone else's copyrighted work.

Exempted Uses

In many instances the ambiguities of the fair use doctrine are resolved by statutory exemptions. Exempted uses apply in situations in which the public interest in making a copy outweighs the potential harm to the copyright proprietor.

Perhaps the most significant of these exemptions is the library and archives exemption, which basically provides that libraries and archives may reproduce and distribute a single copy of a work provided that (1) such reproduction and distribution is not for the purpose of direct or indirect commercial gain; (2) the collections of the library or archives are available to the public or available to researchers affiliated with the library or archives as well as to others doing research in a specialized field; and (3) the reproduction and distribution of the work includes a copyright notice.

In the legislative history of the Copyright Act, Congress encouraged copying of films made before 1942 because these films are printed on nitrate film stock, which decomposes in time. Therefore, as long as an organization is attempting to preserve our cultural heritage, copying old films is allowed and encouraged under the fair use doctrine.

The exemption for libraries and archives is intended to cover only single copies of a work. It does not generally cover multiple reproductions of the same material, whether made on one occasion or over a period of time, and whether intended for use by one person or for separate use by the individual members of a group. Under interlibrary arrangements, various libraries may provide one another with works missing from their respective collections, unless these distribution arrangements substitute for a subscription or purchase of a given work.

This exemption in no way affects the applicability of fair use, nor does it apply where such copying is prohibited in contractual arrangements agreed to by the library or archives when it obtained the work.

CHAPTER 13
Trademarks

■ TRADEMARKS MAY BE USED by gallery owners and crafts retailers to identify work that meets their standards of quality, and to protect their business identities. For example, many famous businesses, such as Tiffany, have protected marks that identify those works bearing such identification as being of a quality acceptable to that business. A unique name, symbol, or logo that identifies an art gallery or craft retail shop may also be a protectible trade or service mark.

Although modern trademark law is a relatively new development, its historical antecedent is found in medieval England. Craft guilds often required their members to place their individual marks on the products they produced so that if a product proved defective, the guild could trace it back to the responsible craftsman. Thus, the use of marks enabled the guild to maintain the integrity of its name. Merchants also would often affix marks to their products so that, should a product be stolen or misplaced, the merchant could prove ownership through the identifying mark.

The use of marks for purposes of identification would no doubt have worked quite well in an ideal society where all the citizens led principled and moral lives. But such was not the case. It's not surprising that unscrupulous merchants quickly realized there was easy money to be made from the use of another's mark, or one confusingly similar. Shoddy merchants could more readily sell their products by affixing to them the marks belonging to quality manufacturers.

In response to this problem of consumer fraud, the first trademark laws developed in the United States in 1870. Initially the emphasis was to prevent one person from passing off his or her product as that of another through the intentional use of a similar mark. Modern U.S. law focuses upon whether one mark is sufficiently similar to another to cause confusion in the minds of the buying public.

Despite these changes, the essential purpose of trademarks and trademark laws has changed little since the days of the craft guilds. Trademarks still function primarily as a means of identifying the source of a particular product. Trademark laws are designed to enable the trademark proprietor to develop goodwill for the product as well as to prevent another party from exploiting that goodwill—regardless of whether that exploitation is intentional or innocent.

What Is a Trademark?

A *trademark* is defined as any word, name, symbol, device, or any combination thereof, adopted and used by a person in commerce—or which a person has a bona fide (good faith) intention to use and subsequently does—that identifies and distinguishes his or her goods from those manufactured or sold by others, and indicates the source of those goods, even if that source is unknown.

A *service mark* is similar to a trademark, although it is used to identify the source of a service, such as art or craft sales, rather than a product. The trademark laws treat service marks in the same way as trademarks, and lawyers lump both under the term "trademarks" or the professional slang, "marks".

A trademark owner may be a licensee, broker, or distributor. The phrase "use in commerce" means the bona fide use of a mark in the ordinary course of trade—rather than simply reserving the right to a mark. You can reserve a mark prior to its use by filing an intent-to-use application with the Patent and Trademark Office (PTO). The key concept is that the trademark must be distinguishable. In order to secure trademark protection, one must devise a distinctive mark.

The most distinctive marks are those that are purely arbitrary or fanciful, that is, those that have no meaning or connotation other than identifying the source of a particular product. For example, the trademark Kroma to identify dichroic glass jewelry is purely arbitrary. Less distinctive are trademarks that have another meaning, such as the trademark Shell to identify gasoline. Although such trademarks as Shell are not purely arbitrary, they are nevertheless afforded substantial protection because the other meaning bears no resemblance to the product identified.

Generic, Descriptive, and Prohibited Trademarks

Generic and descriptive trademarks are not considered distinctive. A generic trademark merely identifies the product for what it is. For example, the use of the trademark Beer to identify beer is generic. Similarly, a descriptive mark merely characterizes the attributes or qualities of the product. For example, the trademark Raisin Bran simply describes the ingredients of the cereal it identifies.

Generic marks are never afforded trademark protection. In the *Leathersmiths of London* case in the mid-1980s, the question was whether the name Leathersmiths of London was a protected trademark. The court held that the word *leathersmith* is generic, and describes someone who is in the business of working with leather and, therefore, is not entitled to trademark protection.

Descriptive trademarks, however, may be protected in limited circumstances. A descriptive mark may be protected if the proprietor of the mark can prove that the mark has acquired a secondary meaning, that is, when the public no longer connects the words of the trademark with their literal meaning, but rather with a unique product. For example, *The Crafts Report* has probably acquired a secondary meaning as the mark of a particular publication that contains topical articles about business, legal, and marketing issues in the crafts industry.

Some trademarks, even though distinctive, are nevertheless prohibited by statute or public policy if they are obscene, scandalous, or derogatory. In 1992, a group of Native Americans petitioned to have registration of the mark "Washington Redskins" canceled on the basis of its being derogatory toward Native Americans. Similarly, trademarks that are deemed deceptive and misleading, such as the mark Idaho Potatoes to identify potatoes produced in an area other than Idaho, are also denied protection.

Protecting a Trademark

Common law is that body of law developed from court decisions rather than from state or federal statutes. Greater protection is secured through federal or state registration, but common-law protection will suffice and has the benefit of not requiring any interaction with governmental agencies.

In order to secure trademark protection, it is not sufficient merely to adopt a distinctive mark. The trademark must actually be used in commerce. The use requirement is fundamental to trademark law and is necessary for common-law protection as well as federal and state registration. A trademark is considered in use when it has been placed in any manner on the product or its containers or the displays associated with it, or on any of the tags or labels affixed to the product.

As long as the trademark is associated with the product at the point of sale and in such a way that the product can be readily identified as coming from a particular manufacturer or source, the trademark may be protected. The mere listing of a trademark in a catalog, the ordering of labels bearing the trademark, the use of the trademark on invoices, or the exhibition of trademarked goods at a trade show may not be sufficient in and of themselves to constitute use. To ensure trademark protection, the trademark proprietor would be well advised to physically affix the trademark to the product, so that it is certain to bear the trademark when it is sold.

Common law protects a trademark proprietor against someone else's later use of a trademark that is confusingly similar. Generally, trademarks will be confusing if they are similar in sound or appearance, particularly if the trademarks are affixed to similar products or if products are marketed throughout the same or similar geographic areas.

On the other hand, if two products bearing similar trademarks are marketed in different geographic areas or are not related products, there may not be any infringement. A business that distributes its products solely in the Northwest could probably adopt and use a trademark already used by a business distributing its product solely in the state of Maine, provided the mark of the Northwest business does not adversely affect the value of the trademark used by the Maine company. A Northwest toy manufacturer could probably adopt and use a trademark used by a Northwest chainsaw manufacturer. It is not likely that the use of the mark by the toy manufacturer would confuse the chainsaw purchasers, although appropriation of another's trademark may be wrongful if the use, even by a noncompeting business, would dilute the value of the mark to the original owner.

Registration with the Principal Register

The federal statute governing trademarks is known as the Lanham Act of 1946. The Lanham Act does not grant trademark rights, because those are secured by the common law principles already discussed; rather it provides a central clearinghouse for existing trademarks via official registration. There are two official registers for trademarks: the Principal Register and the Supplemental Register (p. 72). Application for registration on the Supplemental Registry is only made when registration on the Principal Registry is denied because of some irregularity that prevents registration on the Principal Registry.

In November 1989, the Trademark Law Revision Act (TLRA) of 1988 became effective and made substantive changes to the skeleton of the law provided by the Lanham Act. Prior to the TLRA, a mark could be registered only upon actual use in interstate commerce. This requirement was satisfied when an applicant sold a few units of the product bearing the trademark in an interstate transaction. In fact, a mark could be reserved for later use by making a token use at the time of application. This token-use requirement allowed the registration of trademarks that might never be used, possibly prevented other proprietors from legitimately using the mark, and clogged the federal register with unused marks.

Under the TLRA, token use is no longer necessary or permitted. Actual use of the mark is required in order for a trademark to be registered. In addition, the new law allows for the filing of an application for a trademark based on a bona fide intention to use that mark in the future. This reserves and protects a mark for a limited time and to a limited extent prior to its being used in commerce. If the mark is not actually used, the trademark registration will be denied.

Applications Based on Actual Use

Once the proprietor has established a mark's actual use in commerce, the mark can be registered by filing an application with the PTO. This process entails filling out an application, sending in a drawing of the mark, including specimens of the mark used in commerce, and paying the required fee, currently $210 per category. If the examining officer at the PTO accepts the application, the trademark will appear shortly thereafter in the *Official Gazette*. Anyone who believes that they would be injured by the issuance of the registration has 30 days to file a written notice stating their reasons for opposition. If nobody objects, or if the objections are found to be without merit, a certificate of registration is issued. (For a list of items to include in a trademark or service mark application, **see p. xx, Appendix H.**)

Applications Based on Intent to Use

Under the TLRA, a right to a particular mark can be preserved for future use through the so-called intent-to-use provision. An intent-to-use application should not be made merely for the purpose of reserving a mark. The good faith of the applicant to eventually use the mark in commerce will be determined from the circumstances surrounding the application and the applicant's conduct with respect to the mark.

If the intent-to-use application satisfies the requirements of the PTO regulations, it will receive approval for publication in the *Official Gazette*. Upon publication, a 30-day period for opposition to registration of the mark begins. Those applications that go unopposed receive a "Notice of Allowance". The date the Notice is issued is very important, because the reservation of the mark is limited to a period of six months from the date of allowance, during which period actual use of the mark in commerce must begin or the trademark application will lapse.

If an applicant fails to commence using the mark in commerce within the allowable six-month period, it is possible to obtain an extension for another six months. If submitted before the original six-month period expires, the extension is automatic upon application and payment of fee. Four additional six-month extensions are also possible, but—in addition to an application and fee submitted before the current six-month period expires— these extensions require a showing of good cause as to why the extension should be granted, subject to the approval of the PTO. In no event shall the period between the date of allowance and the commencement of use of the mark in commerce be permitted to exceed 36 months.

In making a request for extension, the applicant must include the following: a verified statement of continued bona fide intent-to-use the mark in commerce; specification as to which classification(s) of goods and services the intent continues to apply; and the required fee, which is currently $100 per extension, per classification of goods or services. (Application forms may be obtained by calling the PTO at (703) 308-0928.)

Once the mark begins to be used in commerce, the applicant must file a Verified Statement of Use. If everything is in order, the mark will be registered for the goods or services that the statement of use indicates. The Commissioner of the PTO shall notify an applicant as to whether the statement of use has been accepted or refused. An applicant will be allowed to amend the statement of use if the mark was not used on all the goods initially identified.

The TLRA generally prohibits assignment of intent-to-use applications, which prevents individuals from applying for marks that they then intend to sell. An intent-to-use application may be assigned from an applicant to the applicant's business, however.

Constructive Use

Under the doctrine of constructive use, the filing of an application to register a mark constitutes use of the mark as of the filing date. Thus, when the application is filed, a right of priority to exclusive use of the mark is created throughout the United States. (The constructive-use doctrine only applies to applications on the Principal Register, not to domestic or foreign applications on the Supplemental Register.)

This doctrine creates a strong incentive to file for registration as early as possible in that it provides priority filing protection, which prevents others from acquiring the mark by simply using it before the applicant does. Constructive use greatly reduces disputes as to which party has priority, thus saving costs and limiting uncertainty in infringement or opposition proceedings.

Exceptions to the priority right of use are marks used prior to the applicant's filing date, intent-to-use applications filed prior to the applicant's filing date; and actual use applications registered prior to the applicant's filing date. Another exception is an application for registration filed by a foreign applicant, if the foreign application was filed prior to the constructive-use application.

Registration on the Supplemental Register

Registration on the Supplemental Register provides protection for individuals capable of distinguishing their marks from those of others, but whose marks do not comply with the requirements for registration on the Principal Register. Supplemental Register applications may be made directly if the applicant is sure that registration on the Principal Registry is unlikely, as, for example, when a mark is merely descriptive and has not achieved a secondary meaning, or if the PTO has refused to register the mark on the Principal Register.

Marks for the Supplemental Register are not published for, or subject to, opposition. They are, however, published as registered in the *Official Gazette*. If a person believes that he or she will be damaged by the registration of another's mark on the Supplemental Register, he or she may at any time petition for cancellation of the registration.

Applications filed on the Supplemental Register cannot be based on intent-to-use and do not enjoy the benefits of constructive use. Under the Lanham Act, an application filed on the Supplemental Register had to be for a mark in lawful use for a year prior to the filing of the application. For a mark to be eligible for registration on the Supplemental Register under the new act, the applicant's mark merely must be in lawful use in commerce, meaning a bona fide use in the ordinary course of trade.

Benefits of Registration

The first benefit is that registration enables the proprietor to use the symbol ® or the word "trademark," in conjunction with their mark, which may deter others from using it. Commonly, TM for trademark or SM for service mark is used in conjunction with an unregistered mark during the application period. These designations have no official status, but they do provide notice to others that the user is claiming a property right in the mark. Proprietors of marks that have not been registered are prohibited from using these symbols.

A second benefit is that registration on the Principal Register is established evidence of the validity of the registration, the registrant's ownership of the mark, and the exclusive right to use the mark on identified goods in commerce.

Third, a registered trademark that has been in continuous use for five consecutive years generally becomes incontestable. By registering the trademark, the proprietor may secure rights superior to those of a prior but unregistered user, if the original user does not object to the registrant's use within five years.

Under the current trademark law, registration remains in effect for a period of ten years, and may be renewed in additional ten-year increments by filing an application for renewal at least six months prior to the expiration of the existing ten-year term. Registrations issued prior to November 16, 1989, received a first-term registration of twenty years, with subsequent registrations to be for ten-year renewals. Those registrations that issue from applications filed with the PTO and that were pending as of November 16, 1989, will have a first term of only ten years, even though filed under the old law.

Obviously, registration of a trademark can be quite beneficial to a manufacturer who has invested time, money, and energy in developing a reputation for quality work. Procuring trademark protection on either the state or federal level may require a considerable amount of time and skill. Also, the total costs for trademark registration usually run about $1,000, not counting any artist's fees for drawings. You'll find that an attorney who specializes in trademarks will be invaluable to you. He or she will be able to help you determine whether the benefits to be derived from registration justify the expenses. Also, your attorney can determine if there are any similar marks in existence, complete the application, and deal with any problems that may occur during its processing.

For attorneys who specialize in trademark work, consult the yellow pages of the telephone directory (look under Patent Agents or Trademark Attorneys), or ask your state bar association for some suggestions.

Loss of Trademark Protection and Infringement

Some forms of use may result in the loss of a trademark. A number of well-known trademarks such as Aspirin, Thermos, and Escalator have been lost as a result of improper usage. Generally, trademark protection is lost because the mark is used in some way other than as an adjective modifying a noun. For example, the mark Xerox is in danger of becoming generic because it is being improperly used when, for example, people state that they are "xeroxing" a document. Customarily, the corporation vigorously polices misuse, pointing out that documents are "photocopied" using a Xerox machine. When a trademark is used as a noun or a verb, it no longer functions to identify the source of the product, but rather becomes the name of the product itself. At that point, the mark becomes generic and not subject to protection.

Abandonment of a mark will also result in loss of protection. A trademark is deemed abandoned when it has not been used for two years and there is no intent to resume its use. Token use is not sufficient to avoid abandonment. To avoid abandonment, the mark must be used in intrastate commerce.

Infringement

The proprietor of a trademark in use that has been infringed can sue the infringing party either for monetary damages or for an injunction pro-

hibiting the infringing use, or sometimes both. Monetary damages may be measured either by the plaintiff's losses resulting from the infringement or by the defendant's profits. In certain exceptional circumstances, where the defendant's conduct is willful and flagrant, the plaintiff might also be entitled to punitive or exemplary damages and/or attorney's fees.

The relevant sections under the laws allow remedies for infringement on marks that are in use. This precludes an intent-to-use applicant from suing for infringement because the applicant has not yet used the mark. The new law permits anyone to sue for unfair competition if they feel they will be damaged by marks that are likely to cause confusion, mistake, or deception as to the origin, sponsorship, or approval of the complainant's goods or services with those of another. Under the new act, TLRA, all remedies available for infringement actions are also available for actions of unfair competition, such as injunctive relief, damages, and attorney's fees.

State Registration

Trademarks can also be registered under state law. The trademark proprietor may file with the appropriate state officer, generally the Secretary of State, a trademark application, along with drawings of the mark and specimens of the mark used in commerce—as required by the Lanham Act. The number of specimens of the mark needed to complete registration may vary from state to state, and the registration fee may also be different.

State protection of a trademark does not extend beyond the borders of the state, but the protection may be broader than that offered by federal law. A federally registered mark may not be infringed by another's use of a similar mark unless there is a likelihood of confusion. Under the state law of many states, however, if the unauthorized use results in a dilution of the value of the protected mark, there is a violation, even if there is no likelihood of confusion. For example, under the federal statute, Lexus, the mark for a model of car, has been held not to infringe the registered mark of a legal research database, Lexis, although an antidilution suit might be successful under state law. Remedies available under state law are also likely to differ from those available under the federal statute. It is important to remember, however, that under the supremacy clause of the U.S. Constitution, if a conflict arises between federal and state trademark law, state law will be preempted in favor of federal law.

CHAPTER 14
Advertising

■ A HOST OF LEGAL ISSUES arise when planning an advertising program. A business may tout the qualities of its products or services in its ads or promotions, but those representations must be true. Most states have consumer protection laws, which, among other things, impose fines and other legal sanctions on businesses that engage in misleading advertising. The state attorney general can also cause an offending advertisement to be withdrawn—as in the case of the false claim of art auctions that the work being auctioned had been created "by starving artists". If your business activity extends beyond your state boundaries and either touches or affects another state, the Federal Trade Commission has jurisdiction over the advertising practices of your business.

When preparing an advertising program, work with an attorney skilled in advertising law to ensure that you have an effective program for selling your product or service that will not violate the rights of other businesses or individuals and expose your business to potential liability. A poorly drafted advertising program is likely to be more harmful than none at all.

Comparative Advertising

It has become quite common for businesses to assert the merits of their products and services by comparing them to those of their competitors. A business is permitted to use the name of a competitor and describe the competitor's products in an ad—even though the comparison will likely point out the competing product's or service's in-feriority—as long as there is no likelihood a consumer would believe that the advertiser is selling the competing product or service, and as long as the statements made are accurate.

In a leading case, it was held that it was permissible for an advertiser to use the names of famous perfumes in an ad that stated that the consumers who like those perfumes will also like the advertiser's less expensive product. The court felt that there was no possibility that the consumer would be misled into believing that the expensive perfume manufacturer was advertising a cheaper, "knockoff" scent. In addition, because the perfumes smelled the same, the statements made were felt to be accurate.

A closely related situation arises when an advertiser intentionally or negligently makes untrue, disparaging remarks about the product or service of another business. In this case, the advertiser may be held legally accountable to the injured party. In a landmark case, a famous art critic stated that a particular painting was a forgery, and as a result, the sale of that painting fell through. The critic was sued successfully for the lost profits of the painting's owner.

For a disparaging remark to be actionable, it must be both untrue and believed by a reasonable person. If the statement made is so outlandish as to be unbelievable, it is likely that the company whose product was disparaged will not be able to prove any injury. For example, if a craft retailer claimed that its competitor's products were so poorly constructed that they literally fell apart within the first week of use, this gross exaggeration would most likely not be actionable.

Right of Publicity and Right of Privacy

A company may use a celebrity to endorse its product, provided the celebrity consents to the endorsement. If not, the company may be liable to the celebrity for violating his or her right of publicity. The right of publicity is granted to those who commercially exploit their names, voices, or images, such as actors, singers, or the like. When manufacturers used look-alikes of Jackie Onassis, Woody Allen, and the rap group The Fat Boys for commercial purposes, liability was imposed.

People who have not achieved notoriety because of their commercial activities may have a right of privacy. Thus, if a person's name or likeness is used in an advertisement without permission, the person may have a claim. In one case, several employees of a bank were photographed while engaged in their day-to-day work. These photographs were displayed as part of the bank's promotional material for a trade show. When the employees, who were given the day off to attend the trade show, saw their photos, they retained an attorney who filed suit. One might conclude from this case that it is dangerous to give employees a day off so that they can attend trade shows, but a more prudent conclusion would be that even bank employees who are not entertainers must grant permission for their names, voices, or likenesses to be used for advertising purposes.

If an individual's photograph is not the focal point of the ad, but rather an incidental part—such as a head in a crowd or a member of an audience—then the individual's permission may not be required before the photograph can be used in an ad. It's a good idea, however, to get a signed photo release whenever possible. The release should be worded in such a way as to give your business permission to use the name and likeness or, if relevant, the person's voice, for any and all purposes, including advertising your business. This will protect you if, for example, the individual eventually becomes well known, and you decide to use the photos that you obtained before the person became a star.

Use of Another's Trademark

An advertiser may use the name or logo of another business within an ad as long as there is no likelihood that the consumer would believe the ad was sponsored by the company whose name or logo is being used. Therefore, it would be permissible for your gallery's ad to contain a photo of an opening with patrons holding bottles of Coca-Cola, as long as it is clear from the advertisement that the Coca-Cola Company is not writing the ad. Similarly, a video advertisement may show a craft shop's delivery vehicle streaking through a metropolitan area and passing by several famous businesses.

Locations

Items of utility, such as buildings, parks, and other landmarks, are not copyrightable, so they may be used in advertising programs without the owner's permission. A business, therefore, could advertise its product with a photograph of someone standing in front of the Empire State Building or the World Trade Center, for example.

Trade Dress

Package design, as a form of advertising, has been given special protection. Although the copyright laws do not protect functional items, such as a product's packaging, the courts have developed a form of protection known as trade dress. The design elements of a particular packaging design are protectable as long as they are not also functional—for example, as a lid or hanger.

The trade dress form of protection is automatic. Blue Mountain Greeting Card Co. developed a distinct and very identifiable line of greeting cards. These cards became quite well known and commercially successful. The Hallmark Greeting Card Company then designed a line of cards that were not identical to those of Blue Mountain, but, in essence, appropriated the look and feel of the Blue Mountain cards. They were so similar that consumers would believe that the Hallmark cards were merely an extension of Blue Mountain's line. For this reason, the court held Hallmark liable for infringing on Blue Mountain's trade dress in the cards. The trade dress doctrine has been extended beyond traditional packaging, and has been used in a variety of cases including the copying of a business's distinctive theme, wearable art, and a craft trade show's theme.

Individuals, too, can have distinctive styles that are protected. A Californian advertiser hired one of Bette Midler's backup singers to replicate Ms. Midler's distinctive vocal rendition of a song for a commercial. Ms. Midler sued and recovered for the knockoff because the intentional copying of the singer's famous, distinctive style and voice was a form of infringement. The California statute protects, among other things, a celebrity's voice. When, however, a manufacturer hired a group that looked and sounded like the rap group known as The Fat Boys, New York's federal court only held the manufacturer liable for violating the celebrities' publicity rights. The New York publicity statute merely extends protection to one's "name, portrait, or picture".

CHAPTER 15
Customer Relations

■ JUST AS WHEN DEALING with artists, the gallery owner or crafts retailer has certain rights and obligations when dealing with customers. In this chapter, I'll discuss several legal aspects of the relationship between you and your customers. For example, what should you do when you suspect a customer of theft? What is your responsibility to a customer who has left an item with you to be framed, mounted, or restored? What is your liability for misrepresentation made by your sales clerks or other agents? What disclosures must you make, by law, to purchasers of editioned art?

Dealing with Shoplifters

An art gallery that shows very large pieces of art work and has an elaborate security system is unlikely to have a problem with shoplifters. Crafts retailers and art galleries that display small items, however, should be particularly attentive to the possibility of theft.

When you suspect a person of theft, you must be very careful to determine that theft has actually occurred. A business person has the right to detain a person reasonably suspected of theft or failure to pay only long enough to investigate the suspected theft. Courts suppose that honest persons should be willing to help clear up any misunderstanding in this short period of time. If you detain a suspected thief against his or her will, you may be liable for false imprisonment. Also, you may not threaten, coerce, or publicly accuse the suspect. In most states, the suspected

thief must be detained before he or she has left the business premises. Of course, if the suspected person has actually stolen goods, there is no liability for having detained the thief.

Proper Care of a Customer's Item

The term *bailment* defines the legal arrangement where one is lawfully in possession of the property of another. Art galleries and crafts retailers who provide framing or mounting or who conduct art restoration are *bailees* of the works in their possession for such services. The owner of the work is the *bailor.*

The bailee (gallery or shop) is obligated to take reasonable care of the work while it is in its possession and to return it to the bailor (owner) in at least as good condition as it was in when it was received. If the work is not returned in at least its original condition, the bailee will probably be liable for negligence. The bailee may retain the work until it receives full payment for any services rendered at the bailor's request in connection with that work. This retention of possession is known as a *possessory lien.* If the obligation is not paid in a reasonable time, the lien may be foreclosed and the property sold to satisfy the debt. The procedure for perfecting and foreclosing liens varies from state to state, and you should consult with a knowledgeable business lawyer before engaging in this type of transaction.

Responsibility for Your Agents

The gallery owner or crafts retailer is responsible for making sure customers know the extent of agents' authority or accept responsibility for any misrepresentations the agents might make to the customer. The relationship between an art gallery or crafts retail shop and its employees is covered by the law of "agency," set forth in the Restatement (Second) of the Law of Agency. Under these rules, the employer is known as the "master" and the employee is typically known as the "servant". The master will be held liable for the servant's wrongful acts when they occur within the scope of employment.

If an employee misrepresents the quality, value, or other attributes of a work of art or craft, the gallery or shop is liable to the buyer for the misrepresentation. The employer may ultimately hold the employee responsible for the wrongful act if it was not authorized. Obviously, if the employee is not economically in a position to make good the loss, the employer's rights against the employee may be worthless.

If an employee sells work and absconds with the money received in payment, the gallery or retailer will have recourse against the employee only if he or she can be found and has the resources to cover the loss. Many employers obtain fidelity bonds on employees who handle money or valuable property. A fidelity bond is a guarantee by an insurance company that the company will pay for any loss sustained as the result of wrongful acts of a bonded employee. Your insurance broker should be able to assist you in obtaining bonding.

The gallery or shop's obligation to consumers for the wrongful acts of its employees extends only to those acts that occur within the scope of the employee's authority. Whether an act is considered to be within this scope is determined by the reasonable expectations of the customer, and not by the actual authority granted by the employer. Thus, if a gallery or retailer instructs an employee not to extend credit and if, in flagrant violation of this rule, the employee consummates a credit transaction, the employer is bound to honor the transaction. Once again, the employee may be liable to the employer for breach of duty, but the innocent purchaser cannot be required to rescind the credit transaction.

Transactions that are obviously outside the scope of an employee's authority will not result in employer liability. For example, a gallery or shop will not be responsible for the acts of an employee who loses his or her temper and assaults a customer, unless the employer was aware of the employee's propensity to commit assaults and retained the employee in a position where the employee's volatile temper could lead to customer injury.

Disclosures Regarding Editioned Work

Dealers in editioned work are obligated by law to disclose certain information to help protect buyers from misrepresentations when buying editioned works, such as fine art prints or editioned sculpture. Many states have enacted fine-print statutes. New York and California have enacted "multiples" laws. Generally, these laws require the seller to provide a buyer with a certificate, invoice, or receipt that contains certain specific information regarding the work.

The information required customarily includes:

- The name of the artist and the year the art was created

- Whether or not the edition is limited

- The present status of the plate or mold

- Whether the work has more than one edition and, if so, the edition of the work, as well as the size of the edition

- Whether the edition is posthumous

- Identification of the workshop or foundary where the edition was printed or cast

Most of the statutes also require information on the medium or process used, such as whether the print is an etching, engraving, woodcut, or lithograph, or whether the bronze is hot or cold cast, or whether the dealer does not know. Some states require disclosure of the method of affixing the artist's name to the multiple (whether signed, stamped, engraved, or molded) and provide that, unless disclosed, the number of multiples described as being in a limited edition shall constitute an express warranty that no additional numbered multiples of the same image have been produced. If the edition is limited, further disclosures are required, including the maximum number of releases, both signed and unsigned, the number of proofs allowed, and the total edition size.

The majority of statutes provide that describing the edition as an edition of "reproductions" eliminates the need to furnish further informational details. Unfortunately, only Oregon and North Carolina define "reproduction".

All the states provide that a person violating these disclosure requirements shall be liable for the amount the purchaser paid. All allow for interest from the date of purchase. In the case of a willful violation in California, Hawaii, New York, and Oregon, the purchaser can recover three times that amount. (See p. 120 for a list of state statutes. For a sample form used by an art registry, see p. 141.)

CHAPTER 16
Liquor and Controlled Substance Liability

■ THINK BEFORE YOU POUR. Art gallery owners and craft retailers who serve alcoholic beverages at openings and other social events should be aware of the extent of their legal responsibility for intoxicated guests.

Liability for wrongful acts committed by intoxicated persons was initially imposed only on licensed servers of alcoholic beverages, such as tavern and restaurant owners. Today, however, social hosts and noncommercial providers, such as colleges, churches, hospitals, etc., are also being held liable—and the amount of liability is staggering. In one Michigan case, a tavern owner's insurance company settled a wrongful death claim for over $10 million. An Ohio bar and its owner were sued for $24 million by the widows of two men killed in a head-on collision. In Indiana, Notre Dame University was held liable for $53,000 for its failure to exercise crowd control at a football game after which a drunken fan assaulted another fan in the parking lot.

Liability is dependent on the serving of alcohol to somebody who is obviously intoxicated or under the legal drinking age. This so-called "dram shop" liability grew out of the temperance movement in the United States. In 1859, Wisconsin enacted the first law, which required tavern owners to post a bond to compensate widows and orphans in the event of wrongful death and pay all costs resulting from injuries caused by individuals who were drinking. Other states quickly followed suit and, by the mid-1870s, 11 states had dram shop laws. Today, most states have statutes regarding alcoholic beverage liability.

The liability of social hosts and noncommercial providers for the wrongful acts of their guests is a rather recent development. New Jersey was one of the first states in which a host was held liable. The court said that any loss in the conviviality of social gatherings was more than outweighed by the social interest in preventing drunken driving. After this ruling, almost half of the states have imposed liability on those who do not make their living serving alcoholic beverages.

Maine's liquor liability act is one of the most comprehensive in the country. Its primary purpose is to prevent "intoxication-related injuries, deaths, and other damages". It specifies liability for negligent or reckless service to minors or to individuals who are already visibly intoxicated when served. There is a ceiling on the total damage award of $250,000, as well as some other procedural safeguards. The law permits those who serve liquor to offer proof of their adherence to what is known as "responsible serving practices", which include attendance at a server-education training course and responsible management policies, procedures, and actions. Laws similar to Maine's have also been adopted in other jurisdictions.

In some states, art galleries and craft shops that serve alcoholic beverages at openings may be required to obtain liquor licenses. Some states also require an annual fee and others allow a per-event license. Check with the authorities in your jurisdiction before serving alcoholic beverages to the public. You should also check your lease for contractual restrictions. Even if your jurisdiction does not require a license, you may still be subject to liability for the wrongful acts of intoxicated guests. This liability may also extend to those who use or share controlled substances, such as marijuana, cocaine, or prescription pharmaceuticals.

Insurance may be available for art galleries and craft retailers who serve liquor, but because of the increase in litigation, insurance companies have sharply increased their premiums; some have dropped liquor-liability coverage entirely. In New Hampshire, Minnesota, and Massachusetts, there are state-operated insurance pools that will divide the risk among participating companies so that liability coverage will be available to all commercial servers. It is not clear whether an art gallery or craft retailer would fit into this category. You may wish to contact your insurance broker or state insurance department for more information.

Social host liability is less well defined and somewhat narrower than that imposed on commercial servers. Because the extent of exposure is not clear and the risk is quite high, however, prudent individuals and businesses will take some precautions when dispensing alcoholic beverages.

Try to ascertain the age of anybody to whom you will be serving an alcoholic beverage, and ask for identification from anybody who appears to be under the age of 21. It's somewhat more difficult to identify intoxicated guests, but you should refuse to serve anybody who appears to have had too much to drink. You and your staff should circulate among your guests at social functions and try to determine whether anybody has had too much to drink. You should also serve food along with any alcoholic beverage; food is believed to slow down the body's absorption of alcohol.

It's also a good idea to provide nonalcoholic beverages at any gathering for those who would prefer them. If a guest appears to be tipsy, you might suggest that he or she switch to the nonalcoholic drink. Arrangements should be made for individuals who have had too much to drink to be driven home, either by other guests or by taxi. Make the "one for the road" a nonalcoholic beverage.

CHAPTER 17
Business Insurance

■ THE INSURANCE BUSINESS originated in a London coffeehouse called Lloyd's, sometime in the late seventeenth century. Lloyd's was a popular gathering place for seamen and merchants engaged in foreign trade. As Shakespeare pointed out in *The Merchant of Venice*, great profit can come from a successful sea voyage, but financial disaster can follow just as surely from a loss of ships at sea. From past experience, these merchants knew that despite their greatest precautions, such disaster could strike any one of them.

Through their dealings with the Italians who already had a system of insurance, the merchants had become familiar with the notion of insurance, but there was no organized insurance company in England at that time. So when these merchants were together at Lloyd's, it became a custom to arrange for mutual insurance contracts. Before a ship embarked, the ship's owner passed around a slip of paper that described the ship, its captain and crew, its destination, and the nature of the cargo. Those merchants who wished to be insurers of that particular ship would initial this slip and indicate the extent to which they could be held liable. The slip was circulated until the entire value of the ship and cargo was covered. This method of creating insurance contracts was called *underwriting*.

Today, the term underwriting describes the formation of any insurance contract, regardless of the means employed in consummating it. Lloyd's of London still uses a method similar to that which originated in the coffeehouse, but most other insurance companies secure against loss out of their own financial holdings. The risks

covered by insurance have also changed. The original Lloyd's insurers dealt in maritime insurance only. Now almost anything can be insured—from a pianist's hands to the Concorde jet.

Although your business may not be as perilous as that of the seventeenth-century merchant, it is not altogether free of risks. Even in rural areas you may become the victim of burglary, and the forces of nature—fire, flood, earthquake—are undiscriminating in their targets. If you operate out of your home, you may already have homeowner's insurance, but your homeowner's insurance likely will not cover your commercial activities.

The financial success of a business often rests with one primary individual—the owner. The risk of lost earnings through the sickness or accident of an owner or essential employee is far too often overlooked. In addition, the sale of an art or craft object subjects you to virtually unlimited liability to anyone who may be injured by a work, no matter how careful you may have been in handling it. The potential magnitude of what this could cost you makes even the slightest chance of its occurrence a significant risk.

Many of these risks can be insured against through any number of insurance companies; however, public policy will not permit you to insure something unless you have what is called an insurable interest. To have an insurable interest, you must have a property right, a contract right, or a potential liability that would result in a real loss to you if a given event occurs. This restriction is intended to minimize the temptation to cause the calamity against which you are insured. There is a joke in the insurance industry about two businessmen who meet at a vacation resort. One, when asked about his business, responds that things are "great". His art gallery had a fire and collected $20,000 from the insurance company. The other exclaims, "Think that's good? We suffered a windstorm loss and recovered $50,000!" The first businessman responds, "How do you start a windstorm?"

What Is Insurance

All insurance is based on a contract between the insurer and the insured whereby the insurer assumes a specified risk for a fee, which is called a *premium.* The insurance contract, or *policy,* must contain at least the following: (1) a description of whatever is being insured (the subject matter); (2) the nature of the risks insured against; (3) the maximum possible recovery; (4) the duration of the insurance; and (5) the due date and amount of the premiums.

When the amount of recovery has been predetermined in the insurance contract, it is called a *valued policy.* An unvalued or open insurance policy covers the full value of property up to a specified policy limit.

The insurance industry is regulated by state law. Insurance companies spread the risk among those subject to that risk through the amount of premium paid by each insured. First, the insurance company obtains data on the actual loss sustained by a defined class within a given period of time. State law regulates how the company defines the class. An insurance company may, for example, separate drivers with many accidents from drivers with few.

Next, the company divides the risk equally among the members of the class. Then the company adds a state-regulated fee for administrative costs and profits. Finally, the premium is set for each individual in proportion to the likelihood that a loss will occur to him or to her.

Besides the method of determining premiums, state insurance laws usually specify the training necessary for agents and brokers, the amount of commission payable to them, and the kind of investments the insurance company may make with the premiums.

The Contract

Even the documents that a company uses to make insurance contracts are regulated from state to state. Sometimes the state requires a standard form from which the company may not deviate, especially for fire insurance. A growing number of states stipulate that all forms must be in "plain English"—that is, there must be a specific average number of syllables per word and average number of words per sentence. Because of a federal ruling that insurance contracts are fraudulent if they exceed certain maximum averages, insurance companies have been forced to write contracts that an average person can understand (nevertheless, only insomniacs read insurance forms).

One frequent result of the language that most insurance contracts are written in is that the signed contract may differ in some respect from what the agent may have led the insured person to expect. If you can prove that an agent actually lied, the agent will be personally liable to you for the amount of promised coverage. Every state has an agency responsible for regulating insurance carriers operating within the state.

Most often the agent will not lie, but will accidentally neglect to inform the insured of some detail. For instance, if you want insurance for transporting work being returned to the artist, the agent may sell you a policy that covers transport only in public carriers—although you intended to rent a vehicle and transport the work yourself. In most states, the courts hold that it is the duty of the insured to read the policy before signing. If you neglected to read the clause that limits coverage to a public carrier, you'd be out of luck. Failure to read the policy is considered no excuse.

In other, more progressive states, this doctrine has been considered too harsh. These states will allow an insured to challenge specific provisions in the signed contract to the extent they do not conform to reasonable expectations resulting from promises that the agent made. In the preceding example, it might be considered reasonable to expect that you would be insured when transporting art or crafts in the gallery's custody. If the agent did not specifically bring your attention to this limitation in the contract, odds are that you would have a good chance of not having that limitation apply to you in the event of a loss.

Of course, I would not advise waiting for an agent to point out these unexpected variations, even in the most liberal state. You should read the contract with the agent. If it is unintelligible, ask the agent to list on a separate sheet all the important aspects before signing, and then keep that sheet with the contract.

Reforming the Contract

After the insurance contract has been signed, its terms can be reformed (revised) only to comply with the original agreement from which the written contract may somehow have deviated.

Let's consider the case of a woman who inherited a pearl necklace. An appraiser, apparently hoping for a large fee, misled her and told her the pearls were genuine and therefore worth $60,000. Before having them shipped from the estate, the woman obtained insurance on them in the amount of $60,000, and paid a premium of $2,450. The description of the subject matter stated that the pearls were genuine. When the pearls were ruined after they arrived at the delivery terminal, but before the woman received them, she tried to collect the $60,000.

In the course of the investigation of the accident it was discovered that the pearls were not genuine but cultured pearls, and worth only $61.50. Of course the insured could not collect $60,000 because no genuine pearls were lost or damaged. The worst of it was that she could not collect even $61.50, because the policy did not cover cultured pearls. The court emphasized that for reformation of the contract to be granted, there must have been something either included

or omitted contrary to the intention of both parties. In this case, neither party ever intended to insure cultured pearls, so the court held that there never was an agreement and refused to create a contract insuring cultured pearls.

You might think that, in this case, the insured would at least get back her premium. She argued this, but lost again. The court reasoned that had the pearls been lost in transit instead of being destroyed, the actual value of the pearls would never have come to light. Therefore, the insurance company had indeed assumed the risk of paying out $60,000 and thus was entitled to the premium.

Overinsuring and Underinsuring

The outcome of this case does not mean that if an insured accidentally overvalues goods, he or she will lose coverage. Had the pearls been genuine, but worth only $20,000, the woman would have recovered $20,000. Overinsurance does not entitle one to a recovery beyond the actual value of the goods. The actual value is the amount of insurable interest. To allow a recovery greater than the insurable interest would be to allow people to gamble with insurance policies.

Because you can, at best, only break even with insurance, you might think it would be profitable to underinsure your goods, pay lower premiums, and lose only if the damage exceeds the policy maximum. This has been tried without success.

An insured stated the value of his unscheduled property as $9,950 and obtained insurance on that amount. (*Unscheduled property* refers to an undetermined collection of goods—for example, all a person's clothes and furniture—which may change from time to time.) A fire occurred that caused at least $9,950 worth of damage. The insurance company investigated the claim and determined that the insured owned at least $36,500 in unscheduled property. The company refused to pay on grounds that the insured obtained the insurance fraudulently. The court agreed with the insurance company, stating that the intentional failure to communicate the full value of the unscheduled property rendered the entire contract void. Therefore, the insured could not even collect the policy maximum. All he could hope for at best would simply be to get his premiums back.

Although at first glance this decision may seem harsh, its ultimate fairness becomes apparent with a little analysis. The chance of losing $9,950 out of $36,500 is greater than the chance of losing $9,950 out of $9,950 simply because most accidents or thefts do not result in total losses. In this case, the insured paid premiums for less than the $9,950 coverage because he was in a high-risk category.

The courts have various criteria for determining whether or not an omission or misstatement renders a policy void. In all cases, however, the omission or misstatement must be intentional or obviously reckless, and must be material to the contract. *Materiality* is determined by the degree of importance that the insurance company ascribes to the omitted or misstated fact. If stating the fact correctly would have significantly affected the conditions or premiums that the company would demand, then the fact is material. In the preceding case, had the full value of the unscheduled property been stated, the insurance company would either have required that the full value be insured, or that a higher premium be paid for the limited coverage. Thus, the misstatement was clearly material.

Unintentional undervaluing

Many insurance contracts allow some undervaluation where it is not material and not intentional. This provision is designed to protect the insured from inflation, which causes property to increase in replacement value before the policy's renewal date. Considering the inflation rate, it is wise to reexamine your coverage each year.

A so-called coinsurance clause generally provides that the insured may recover 100 percent of any loss up to the face value of the policy, provided the property is insured for at least 80 percent of its full value. For example, if a gallery worth $100,000 was insured for $80,000 and suffered a $79,000 loss from a covered casualty, the insured would recover the full amount of the loss, or $79,000. If the gallery was only insured for $50,000, a formula would be used to determine the amount of recovery: divide the amount of insurance coverage by the total value of the property; multiply the resulting fraction by the loss.

For example, $50,000 (insurance) divided by $100,000 (value of business), times $79,000 (loss), equals $39,500 (recovery).

You can see why it's important to carry insurance on at least 80 percent of the value of your property.

Scheduling property

All insurance policies are limited to certain defined subject matter and to losses caused to that subject matter by certain defined risks. Once the risks are recognized, it is a simple matter to decide whether to insure against them or not. However, correctly defining the subject matter of insurance is tricky business. Mistakes here are not uncommon and can result in any one of us finding ourselves uninsured—like the woman with the pearl necklace.

The typical insurance policy will include various exclusions and exemptions. For example, most homeowner and auto insurance policies cover personal property but exclude business property. If a gallery owner keeps artwork at home for personal enjoyment, are those pieces personal or business property? The answer depends on whether the person ever sells or displays any of these items. If any are sold or displayed, they may be considered business property.

In order to avoid a potentially tragic loss because of a technicality, the gallery owner may simply schedule the pieces that are held for personal enjoyment. Scheduling is a form of inventorying in which the insured submits a list and description of all pieces to be insured with an appraisal of their value. The insurer assumes the risk of loss of all scheduled works without concern as to whether they pertain to the business or not. Insurance on scheduled property is slightly more expensive than that of unscheduled property.

Many battles occur between the insurer and the insured over the value of objects stolen, destroyed, or lost. In anticipation of such battles, maintain records of sales to establish the market price of your art and craft work and keep an inventory of all works on hand. The value of art or craft work must be determined by an expert in the field—both when the policy is obtained and after a loss—but this will not always prevent the insurance company from contesting the scheduled value.

What and When to Insure

Four factors should be weighed to determine whether or not to obtain insurance. First, you must set a value on that which is to be insured. Life and health are of the utmost value and should always be insured. Material goods are valued according to the cost of replacement. If you keep a large inventory of art or crafts or if you own expensive fixtures, such as display cases, they probably should all be insured. The most elementary way to determine whether the value is sufficiently high to necessitate insurance is to rely on the pain factor: if it would hurt to lose it, insure it.

You should also consider whether it is appropriate for your gallery or shop to obtain "business interruption" insurance or "business overhead expense" insurance. Business interruption insurance is designed to provide the business owner with lost earnings resulting from business interruption caused by specified risks, such as fire, storms, and the like. Business overhead expense insurance provides coverage for the loss or injury of an identified "key person". Customarily, there is a 30-day waiting period after the loss or injury before payments begin, and then a period of approximately two years within which overhead, such as salaries, rent, utilities, and the like, are reimbursed.

Second, you must estimate the chances that a given calamity will occur. An insurance broker can tell you what risks are prevalent in your type of business or in your neighborhood. You should supplement this information with your personal knowledge. For example, you may know that your gallery is virtually fireproof, or that only a massive flood would cause any real damage. Although these facts should be weighed in your decision, you should not be guilty of audaciously tempting fate, for, as the great tragedians have recounted, to scoff at disaster is to invite it. And if the odds are truly slim, but some risk is still present, the premium will be correspondingly smaller in most cases.

The third factor is the cost of the insurance. Bear in mind that insurance purchased to cover your business is tax deductible. That means if you pay tax at a rate of 31 percent, Uncle Sam is theoretically paying for 31 percent of your premium.

Fourth, you must determine whether you are legally obligated to obtain certain insurance. For example, commercial leases customarily require the tenant to maintain liability insurance in specific amounts, with the landlord as an identified insured party. There may be a comparable provision in your mortgage. Some state artist-gallery consignment laws require the art gallery or crafts retailer to insure the consigned work.

Keeping Costs Down

As I've already explained, the premiums charged by an insurance company are determined by state law. Nonetheless, it still pays to shop around. Insurance companies can compete by offering different packages of insurance and by hiring competent agents to assist you in your choice.

Co-op insurance
If there are enough art galleries, craft retailers, or similar businesses in your area, it may be possible for you to form a co-op insurance fund. To do this, you must estimate the total losses your co-op

would sustain in the course of a year. Each member contributes a pro rata share, and the money is put into a bank or other investment to collect interest. If a disaster occurs and the losses are greater than the fund, each member must contribute an additional amount to make up the difference. If there is money left over, it can be applied to the next year's coverage, thereby reducing the premiums for that year. Co-op insurance is cheaper than conventional insurance because it eliminates the insurance agents' commissions and the insurance company's profit. But before you form a co-op insurance fund, contact an attorney to be sure you comply with the regulations in your state.

CHAPTER 18
Product Liability

ALTHOUGH ART GALLERY owners and craft retailers probably rarely think of themselves as liable for defective products, they may be. Every year, seemingly harmless works of art and craft are responsible for numerous injuries. For example, a glass artist sold a luminaria, beveled on one side, to a purchaser who hung it in the window as a sun catcher. Because of the bevel, the glass acted as a prism and started a fire that resulted in more than $500,000 damage. Both the artist who created the work and the gallery that sold it were held responsible for the loss.

To understand the present-day liability law, it's useful to examine its roots. In 1804, a craftsman named Seixas went to a warehouse to buy some braziletto wood, supposedly a valuable wood. Mr. Woods, the warehouseman, sold Seixas peachum wood instead, which is virtually worthless. Neither party, apparently, knew the difference between braziletto and peachum. When Seixas discovered the error, he tried to return the worthless wood in exchange for braziletto or for a refund of his money. Woods refused because he had already given the money to the original owner of the wood. Seixas sued Woods and lost. Even though Woods had written braziletto on the invoice, he never warranted the wood as such.

This case can be aptly summed up in the Latin maxim *caveat emptor:* let the buyer beware. This maxim has been proven true time and again in both English and American court cases. Gradually, however, the pendulum began to swing the other way, and now the rule is *caveat seller:* let the seller beware.

One of the harshest rules of early product liability cases was that only individuals who dealt with each other could have rights against each other. Injured consumers could not sue manufacturers unless the defective products were purchased directly from them; consumers could only sue the retailer with whom they had traded. So early on, the pattern was established that dealers were liable for injuries sustained as a result of defective products they sold. The current product-liability law holds the producer as well as the seller of a product liable.

An art gallery owner or craft retailer might have the right to seek indemnification from the artist or craftsperson who created the defective work, but there are some practical limitations. For example, if the artist is insolvent or cannot be found, an indemnification claim may be worthless. Similarly, if the defect cannot be traced to the artist or maker—for example, a crack in a piece of pottery that could have occurred in the gallery or shop—no indemnification will be available.

The seller, regardless of his position in the chain of distribution, could be sued if he were negligent or if the product were "inherently dangerous". The courts struggled for some time over just what was and what was not inherently dangerous. Justice Benjamin Cardozo, in a landmark case involving the safety of an automobile, ruled that a product was inherently dangerous if injury to the owner was predictable in cases where the item was defective. Almost anything can be injurious if defective. Negligence suits have been brought for such seemingly innocuous items as a glazed mug, an art glass vessel, and a piece of kinetic art.

This shift of the burden of responsibility from the buyer to the seller was a natural response to several factors. First, as products became increasingly more complex, it was no longer true that the buyer and seller were equally knowledgeable or ignorant. Second, it was felt that businesses were large enough to bear the immediate losses and ultimately could spread the risk over an even broader sector of society.

Because the majority of the products on today's market are mass-produced by large manufacturers, the present rule reflects the economic reality of industry. This is not, however, the economic reality of the fine arts and crafts markets, but you must learn to cope with these laws in a climate of litigious consumers and generous juries. It is better to learn about these problems while you can still protect yourself than when it is too late.

Types of Liability

In every product liability case, the plaintiff must prove that: (1) some injury occurred to him or her; (2) the injury was caused by some defect in the product; and (3) the defect was present in the product when the defendant had control over it. You cannot control the first two conditions: Once a person takes possession of the product sold by you, you cannot stop him or her from being injured. You can, however, control this third condition by making sure that any item you sell is without defect.

There are two kinds of defects: mechanical defects, such as loose screws, faulty component parts, and so on; and design defects, such as instability, flammability, toxicity, tendency to shatter, etc.

Liability for Mechanical Defects

The scrupulous attention to detail that is usually characteristic of handcrafted goods almost precludes the possibility of a mechanical defect. If there is a mechanical defect, it will most likely occur in a component produced by someone else.

For example, a stained glass lamp might contain a faulty electrical circuit that could cause serious injury to a user. Such a defect would be virtually impossible to detect. But, under the current rule of "strict liability", followed by most states, you can be held liable for defects that could not have been discovered or prevented by human skill, knowledge, or foresight. In this case, your protection is either insurance or your ability to sue the artist for indemnification, if that person can be found and is solvent.

If the right types of tests are made, many defects are detectable before an accident occurs. The courts have held that manufacturers (corporate or individual) have a duty to inspect and test their goods. Failure to adequately test has been held reason enough to impose large awards of punitive damages in addition to the actual damages.

Sophisticated testing procedures might prove to be too expensive for art gallery owners or crafts retailers, but it would be prudent to require the artist or crafts person to provide you with test results, if possible. I also advise you to design the best test you can for whatever you sell, even if it is only a good tug here and there and, most important, to keep a record of the test and its result. This may serve to prove that you attempted to fulfill your duty to test the product. While this precaution might not protect you from product liability, it may result in reducing, if not eliminating, punitive damage awards against you. Rarely can an injured plaintiff prove that a defect was present when a product was purchased, and must rely instead on inferences from the accident itself. If the jury is convinced that there is more than a fifty-fifty chance that the defect was there when the product was bought, the plaintiff will probably win. But, if you come into court with a record of tests on your products, the odds might shift in your favor.

Design Liability

Design defects can be divided into two categories: those that are and those that are not a violation of a statute. A 1959 case contains a good example of how far a court might go in defining a design defect. A rather obese woman entered a store and sat in a chair of contemporary design that the store had on display for sale. The back of the chair curved elegantly into the seat, which in turn curved down and around to form the base of the chair. It was along these serpentine curves that the overweight customer slid onto the floor. The injury to her pride was aggravated by an injury to her spine. The court held that the shape of the chair was defective and awarded her $25,000 in damages.

In cases to determine liability for defective design, the courts have usually adhered to a common-sense criterion. If the product conforms to the state of the art when it was made, it will usually not be held defective. The state-of-the-art standard is the measure of how far technology in the field has advanced. The state-of-the-art standard is not the same as industry-wide standards. Industry-wide standards may be introduced in evidence, but it cannot be assumed that these assure due care or adherence to state-of-the-art standards. The law will not allow an industry to adopt careless practices in order to save money or time when better, more protective methods are available.

A design may be defective if it does not meet the standards set forth in a statute. Some products are also covered by consumer protection law. A violation of these laws may carry criminal sanctions. In some jurisdictions, consumers injured by a product have proven their case merely by proving that a statute was violated in the production or sale of the product. The manufacturer then bears the burden of establishing that the injury was not the result of the statutory violation, which would be almost impossible in cases where the law had been enacted to prevent the very type of injury claimed. For example, putting small, lovely fastener beads on infants toys in violation of state child safety laws for such toys would expose the toymaker, as well as the dealer who sold the toy, to liability if an infant choked on the bead.

Federal Laws

In addition to state legislation, there are at least three federal laws regarding liability that directly affect artists and craftspeople. The first is the Hazardous Substance Labeling Act, as amended by the Child Protection Act of 1966 and the Child Protection and Toy Safety Act of 1969. These statutes were passed in response to the staggering number of injuries and poisonings each year of children under age fifteen. Under the Hazardous Substance Labeling Act as amended, the Federal Trade Commission (FTC) is empowered to name any potentially dangerous substance a hazardous substance. Such substances may not be used in any product that a child may have access to—that is, no amount of use or abuse by a child should make the product unsafe. Presently banned under this Act, for example, are jaquirty beans used in necklaces, jewelry, and dolls' eyes. (For a list of other hazardous substances, you should consult your local office of the FTC.)

The second federal statute is the Flammable Fabrics Act. This statute empowers the FTC to establish appropriate standards of flammability for fabrics used in clothing and household products, including children's toys.

Finally, there is the Consumer Product Safety Act, a statute that empowers the FTC to regulate the composition, content, and design of consumer products, including works of art and craft. The FTC has, for example, regulations for the use of architectural glass in doors, windows, and walls, and has banned the use of any lead-based surface coating materials (such as paint). This is a very volatile issue, and artists and craftspeople should check with the FTC to determine whether the materials they use in their work are subject to regulation. Galleries and dealers should obtain representations from the artists and craftpeople with whom they deal regarding their compliance with the laws. Although this may not exempt you from liability, if, for example, the artist or craftperson lies, it will likely prevent the imposition of punitive damages.

If You Are Held Liable

If you are held liable for a defective product, you may in turn seek reimbursement from the artist or craftsperson for the amount paid in damages. This may involve another expensive suit, and, if the person you bought the work from is broke, you're out of luck. There are two things that you might do to protect yourself. You can incorporate (see Chapter 1), or you can obtain liability insurance.

In general, liability insurance is affordable for the small business: $100,000 of liability insurance for a person doing up to $10,000 of business a year will cost about $100 annually, although rates will vary. (Consult your insurance broker or agent to determine the rates in your region.) Each dealer must then evaluate this cost against the risks of a lawsuit. You should know that the majority of these suits are settled or adjudicated for more than $100,000. You can claim the cost of this insurance as a business expense for tax purposes.

CHAPTER 19
Renting Commercial Space

ALTHOUGH SOME ART AND CRAFTS sales are made from a dealer's home, the vast majority of work is sold through galleries or shops. And if you're just starting out, you'll likely need to rent commercial space. The terms and conditions of a commercial lease are much more subject to negotiation and pitfalls than residential leases, which are more tightly regulated in most states. Consult an experienced attorney before signing a commercial lease. These are some of the things you'll want to discuss together.

Terms of the Lease

The exact space to be rented should be specified in the lease in detail. If your space is in a shopping center and you share responsibility for common areas with other tenants, these responsibilities should be explained. Will you be responsible for cleaning and maintaining them, or will the landlord? When will the common areas be open or closed? What other facilities are available to you, such as restrooms, storage, etc.?

Another important item to specify is the cost. Will you be paying a flat monthly rent or one that will change based on your earnings at the location, as is often the case when stores lease space in a shopping center? Is there an escalator clause that will automatically increase your rent based on some external standard, such as the Consumer Price Index, or the like? In order to evaluate the cost of the space, compare it with similar spaces in the same locale. Do not be afraid to negotiate for more favorable terms.

If the space you are renting is in a mall that has an "anchor" tenant—for example, a major department store—determine whether your proximity to that business is important to your business. If so, you should negotiate for a provision that enables you to terminate your lease if the anchor tenant leaves and is not replaced by a comparable business.

Also consider the period of the lease. If, for example, you are merely renting a booth at a trade show, you are only concerned with a short term. On the other hand, if you intend to rent for a year or two, it is a good idea to get an option to extend, because when you advertise and promote your business, your location is one of the things you will be telling people about. Moving can cause a lot of problems with the forwarding of mail and changing of telephone numbers. Besides, if you move every year or two, some customers may feel that you are unstable, and infrequent customers may not know where to find you after the lease period ends—worse still, they may find a competitor in your old space.

Long-term leases are recordable in some states. Recording, where permitted, is generally accomplished by having the lease filed in the same office where a deed to the property would be filed. (Check with a local real estate title company or real estate attorney for the particulars in your state.) It's a good idea to record your lease if you can, because then you'll receive legal and other notices that are related to the property.

Find out whether or not there are restrictions on the activity you wish to perform on the leased premises. For example, the area may be zoned so as to prohibit you from engaging in retail sales. Insist on a provision that puts the burden of obtaining any permit or variances on the landlord. Or, if you are responsible for permits and variances, but are unable to obtain them, you should be able to terminate the lease without penalty to you.

Shopping malls frequently have restrictions in their leases designed to prohibit competitive operations. You should determine whether your gallery or craft retail store will sell merchandise that is also available from other stores in the same complex. Be clear about the scope of coverage—for example, craft retailers often handle wearable art and jewelry, which may run afoul of a prohibition against competitive sale of "upscale" clothing handled by boutiques. Don't sign a lease that will restrict you from opening another shop close to the one being rented.

Does the lease have restrictions on the time or location for making or accepting deliveries? If your business requires that you ship or receive large bulky items, your lease should contain a provision that will give you the flexibility you need.

Also be sure the lease provides that you are permitted to use any sign or advertising on the premises, or spells out any restrictions. It is not uncommon, for example, for historic landmark laws to regulate signs on old buildings. Some zoning laws prohibit signs in windows or in front of a building.

Who Pays for What?

You should also be aware that extensive remodeling may be necessary for certain spaces to become suitable for your use. If this is the case, it is important for you to determine who will be responsible for the costs of remodeling. In addition, it is essential to find out whether it will be necessary for you to restore the premises to their original, preremodeled condition when the lease ends. This can be expensive and, in some instances, impossible.

If you need special hookups, such as water or electrical lines, find out whether the landlord will provide them or whether you have to bear the cost. Of course, if the leased premises already have the necessary facilities, you should question the landlord to determine whether their cost is included in the rent or are paid separately.

In some locations, garbage pickup is provided by the municipality, but often renters are responsible for their trash disposal. In commercial areas, this can be quite expensive, so this expense should also be addressed in the lease.

Customarily, the landlord is responsible for the exterior of the building. The landlord is obligated to make sure the building doesn't leak during rainstorms, and that it is properly ventilated. Notwithstanding this fact, it is important that the lease specifies who is responsible if, for example, the building is damaged and some of your inventory or fixtures are damaged or destroyed. Will you have to take out insurance for the building as well as its contents, or will the landlord assume responsibility for building insurance?

You should, of course, have your own liability policy for accidental injuries or accidents that occur on your leased premises. Find out whether you are also obligated to obtain liability insurance for injuries caused in portions of the building not under your control, such as common hallways and stairwells. You may also wish to have business interruption insurance (see p. 87) to cover your losses if, for example, your business is shut down by a natural disaster, such as a hurricane or tornado.

Security and Zoning

A good lease will contain a provision regarding security. If you're renting space in shopping complex, it's likely that the landlord will be responsible for external security, although this is not always the case. If you rent an entire building, it is customarily your responsibility to provide whatever security you deem important. Check that the lease permits you to install locks or alarm systems, if you are interested in having them.

Examine a potential business location carefully to determine exactly what you can do on the premises, and whether or not the landlord or municipal rules will allow you to use the location for your intended purpose.

If you plan to use the rental space as both your personal dwelling and your business location, consult your attorney first. The zoning laws in some jurisdictions permit individuals to live in only certain types of industrially zoned buildings, such as warehouses. Some jurisdictions permit a limited range of commercial activity in residentially zoned areas—for example, light manufacturing businesses, such as a craftsperson's or artist's studio; professional services, such as a lawyer's, doctor's, or accountant's office. Rarely will these zoning exceptions permit ongoing retail activities.

Security Deposits

When the lease is first executed, landlords will often require new tenants to pay the first month's rent, the last month's rent, and a security deposit. Some state laws require landlords to keep security deposits in a special trust account during the term of the lease. These funds are available to the landlord if the tenant causes an injury to the property during the lease or fails to leave the premises in proper condition. Tenants who fulfill all of their obligations under the lease should be entitled to a refund of their deposit when the lease expires.

You should try to negotiate for the landlord to pay interest on all monies held as security as well as on the prepaid last month's rent. Some states require interest to be paid on security deposits.

Most commercial leases require the tenant to pay, and be responsible for all utilities. You should make these arrangements directly with the utility companies. The landlord should not be involved. Because public utilities are tightly regulated, it is highly unlikely that any negotiation between you and the public utility will be fruitful regarding deposits, rates, fees, or contractual arrangements.

Late Rent

All leases require the tenant to pay rent at the beginning of each month. Customarily, a lease will impose a penalty on the tenants for a late rent payment. You should try to negotiate for a fairly long grace period—ten or fifteen business days—before your rent is deemed late. Generally, the late charges are called service charges or something similar to avoid their being characterized as penalties or interest, either of which are subject to specific rules regarding disclosure and amount.

Finally, it is essential that every item agreed upon between you and the landlord is stated in writing. Many state laws provide that a long-term lease is an interest in land and can be enforced only if in writing. The writing may consist of several documents: for example, some shopping malls use a "master lease", which governs the rights and responsibilities of all tenants, as well as an individual lease, which deals only with the issues unique to the specific rental space. In addition to leases, landlords may also add rules and regulations to the lease that are binding on all tenants regarding, for example, parking, waste disposal, rules for common areas, etc.

CHAPTER 20

Tax

■ LIKE ALL BUSINESS PERSONS, gallery owners and crafts retailers must pay taxes on all income, whatever the source or form, whether ordinary income or capital gains. This chapter will focus on federal income tax. You should consult with a tax professional to determine state and other local tax liability as well as your responsibility to collect and pay sales tax.

If you are doing business as a sole proprietor, you'll report your business income on your personal return. A partnership files an informational return, and the partners report their proportional shares of profit or loss on their personal returns. Corporations are required to pay income tax on their taxable income; the shareholder/owners pay taxes only on the dividend income they receive. (Traditionally, corporations were taxed at a lower rate than individuals. In the last decade, however, personal tax rates have been reduced to a lower level than corporations, thereby minimizing the tax advantages of incorporation. There are still some tax advantages, however, and a corporation is still a very viable liability shield in most instances.)

Capital Gains

Net capital gain is defined by the Internal Revenue Code (IRC) as the excess of net long-term capital gain (i.e., the excess of long-term capital gain over long-term capital losses) over net short-term capital losses (i.e., the excess of short-term capital losses over short-term capital gains). Thus, depending on the taxpayer's other gains and losses,

a capital gain generally occurs when he or she sells or exchanges at a gain a capital asset held for more than one year. Capital losses are first used to offset capital gains in the year incurred. Any additional capital losses are deductible from ordinary income up to a maximum amount of $3,000 per year, although any excess losses can be carried forward to the following taxable year.

Traditionally, capital gains were taxed at low rates, creating an incentive to characterize income as capital gains rather than ordinary income. Today, taxpayers in the 31 percent tax bracket realize a three percent tax savings on capital gains income. All other taxpayers pay the same rate on both capital gains and ordinary income.

Because gallery owners and crafts retailers deal almost exclusively in inventory, you generally will not realize capital gains income from your business operations. You might, however, realize a capital gain if a capital asset other than inventory is sold at a profit—for example, buildings, vehicles, fixtures, or, usually, anything with a useful life of more than one year.

Deductions

Once income is characterized as ordinary income or capital gain, you must determine how much of it is taxable. The taxpayer is permitted to deduct certain trade or business expenses to arrive at adjusted gross income (so-called "above the line deductions"). Other itemized deductions are subtracted from adjusted gross income to arrive at taxable income (so-called "below the line deductions"). Taxpayers have no constitutional guarantee of deductions; thus, if there is no specific legislation allowing it, there is no adjustment to gross income.

In order to be deductible, the expense must be incurred in connection with a business rather than for personal reasons. In addition, the taxpayer must show that the expense is "ordinary and necessary" and that it is a current expense rather than a capital investment. Generally, the "ordinary and necessary" requirement is open-ended under IRC 162, and specifically includes a reasonable allowance for salaries or other compensation, traveling expenses, and rentals. Because these types of expenditures create benefits only in the current tax year, they also are current expenses.

IRC 263 disallows deductions for the cost of acquiring property whose useful life extends substantially beyond the close of the taxable year. These, as noted above, are capital investments and, because their cost represents a payment by the taxpayer for economic benefits that will accrue in the future, the deduction must be spread over the theoretical useful life of the property. Thus, expenses incurred to extend the useful life of capitalized property or to alter its function—for example, the installation of heat and humidity controls in a building for art conservation purposes—cannot be deducted as current expenses. Rather, they are added to the property's basis and amortized over time. By contrast, simple repairs and maintenance—such as repairing a chipped frame on a painting—are deductible as current expenses. The amounts paid to your business's lawyer, tax preparer, and other professionals are also deductible.

Losses are deductible when they are incurred in a trade or business, in any transaction entered into for profit, or as a result of fire, storm, shipwreck, other casualty, or theft. Gallery owners and crafts retailers who suffer losses due to a disaster such as a hurricane may qualify for a special tax deduction. If the President of the United States declares the affected areas to be disaster areas qualified for federal assistance, taxpayers may deduct their disaster losses from the previous year's tax liability.

Employee Compensation

For gallery owners or crafts retailers who are doing business as C corporations, payment of employee compensation is actually one of the most effective ways to minimize or eliminate double taxation (see Chapter 1). Rather than paying out corporate earnings to shareholder/employees as nondeductible dividends, the corporation can pay out high salaries and receive a business expense deduction for the wages paid. Although an S corporation is not saddled with the double tax, the shareholders of an S corporation still benefit from a deduction for employee compensation, because it decreases taxable income.

This deduction provides a potentially large loophole in the IRC, which Congress and the courts have all but closed by placing a limit on the amount of deduction—only that which is "reasonable compensation" may be deducted as a business expense. Reasonability, as always, depends on all the circumstances of the particular case. The courts consider factors such as the nature of the job, the size and complexity of the business, prevailing rates of compensation, the company's profitability, the uniqueness of the employee's skills or experience, the number of hours worked, the employee's salary as compared with the salaries of co-workers, general economic conditions, and the presence, absence, and amount of dividends paid.

The IRS frequently audits closely held corporations to determine whether they are attempting to avoid income tax by paying excessive salaries to shareholder/employees. Although most challenges are to salaries and benefits for stockholders, excessive compensation paid to a non-stockholder employee also has been successfully challenged by the Service. If a salary is found to be excessive, no deduction will be allowed for the part of the payment that is excessive. Even though the employer cannot deduct the full amount paid, the employee must report and pay tax on the full amount received.

Usually, a new business is more concerned with underpayment than overpayment. Employees may work long, hard hours with little compensation in the hope of a brighter future. The Service realizes this. In later years, when the business is profitable, employees can be compensated for the underpayment of former years by additions to their salaries. The base salaries and additional amounts must be reasonable in light of the past services performed and the compensation already received.

Compensations also may be fixed as a percentage of profits or earnings. Contingent plans of this nature may result in low salaries in lean years and above-average salaries in good years. The Service accepts this too, as long as, on the average, the salaries are not unreasonable. Of course, some premium is reasonable due to the risk assumed by the employee who accepts such a plan. Contingent plans are suspect, however, when used for owner/employees, because they can be used to avoid dividends in good years. A shareholder/employee's reward for an increase in business should be a reasonable salary and increased dividends.

Hiring Family Members

Business owners in high tax brackets may wish to divert some income directly to members of their immediate families who are in lower tax brackets by hiring them as employees. Adding dependent children to the payroll can result in a substantial tax savings, because their salaries can be deducted as a business expense, but, at the same time, you may not be required to withhold Social Security from the children's wages.

Your child can earn up to the amount of the standard deduction without any tax liability, which, as of the date of this writing, is $5,550. You, as the taxpayer, can still claim a personal-dependency exemption for the child if you provide over half of his or her support. This salary arrangement is permissible as long as the child is under 19 years of age or, if 19 or older, is a full-time student. The child, however, may not claim a personal exemption if he or she can be claimed by the parents on their tax return. There are three other restrictions on this arrangement:

1. The salary must be reasonable in relation to the child's age and the work performed

2. The work performed must be a necessary service to the business

3. The work must actually be performed by the child

Travel and Entertainment Expenses

Gallery owners and crafts retailers frequently travel to shows in order to acquire works for their inventories. On a business trip, whether within the United States or abroad, ordinary and necessary expenses may be deductible if the travel is solely for business purposes. Transportation costs are fully deductible, except for "luxury water travel", as are costs of lodging while away from home on business. As of 1987, only 80 percent of the costs of business meals and meals consumed while on a business trip were deductible.

If the trip is primarily for business, but part of the time is personal vacation, the expenses for business and pleasure must be separated. This is not true in the case of foreign trips, if one of the following exceptions applies:

- The taxpayer had no control over arranging the trip

- The trip outside of the United States was for a week or less, or

- The taxpayer is not a managing executive or shareholder of the employing company

If claiming one of these exceptions, be careful to have supporting documentation. If the exceptions do not apply, then expenses for the trip abroad must be allocated according to the percentage of the trip devoted to business rather than vacation.

The IRS tends to review very carefully any deductions for attendance at business seminars that also involve a family vacation, whether inside the United States or abroad. In order to deduct the business expense, you must be able to show, with documentation, that the reason for attending the meeting was to promote production of income. Normally, for a spouse's expenses to be deductible, the spouse's presence must be required by your employer. If you have organized as a partnership or corporation, it may be advantageous for tax purposes to make your spouse a partner, employee, or member of the Board of Directors of the company.

Whether inside or outside of the United States, the definition of what constitutes "a business stay" is essential in determining a trip's deductibility. Travel days, including the day of departure and the day of return, count as business days if business activities occurred on such days. If travel is outside the United States, the same rules apply if the foreign trip is for more than seven days.

Any day you spend on business counts as a business day even if only a part of the day is spent on business. A day in which business is canceled through no fault of yours counts as a business day. Saturdays, Sundays, and holidays count as business days even though no business is conducted, provided that business is conducted on the Friday before and the Monday after the weekend, or on one day on either side of the holiday.

Entertainment expenses incurred for the purpose of developing an existing business are also deductible, in the amount of 80 percent of the actual cost. You must be especially careful about recording entertainment expenses, however. The amount, date, place, type of entertainment, business purpose, substance of the discussion, the participants in the discussion, and the business relationship of the parties who are being entertained should be recorded. Keep receipts for any expenses over $25. Also keep in mind the stipulation in the Tax Code that disallows deductibility for expenses that are "lavish or extravagant under the circumstances". Unfortunately, no guidelines have yet been developed as to the definition of "lavish or extravagant". If you buy tickets to a sporting, cultural, or other event for business entertaining, only the face value of the ticket is allowed as a deduction. If you purchase or lease a skybox or other luxury box seat, the maximum deduction now allowed is the cost of the non-luxury box seat.

These rules cover business travel and entertainment expenses both inside and outside of the United States. The rules are more stringent for deducting expenses incurred while attending conventions, seminars, and conferences outside the United States. The IRS is taking a closer look at cruise-ship seminars and now requires you to attach two statements to your tax return: the first statement substantiates the number of days on the ship, the number of hours spent each day on business, and the activities in the program; the second statement must come from the sponsor of the convention to verify the information in the first statement. In addition, the ship must be registered in the United States, and all ports of call must be located in the United States or its possessions. Again, the key, if you're taking this sort of deduction, is careful planning, documentation, and substantiation.

Keeping a log book or expense diary is probably the best line of defense with respect to business expenses incurred while traveling. When on the road:

- Keep proof of the costs

- Record the time of departure

- Record the number of days spent on business

- List the places visited and the business purposes of your activities

- Keep copies of all receipts in excess of $25 for transportation, meals, tips, lodging, etc.

- If traveling by car, keep track of mileage

- Log all expenses under $25 in a diary

Donations

Gallery owners and crafts retailers may take a deduction from adjusted gross income for cash donations to certain qualified charitable organizations. The aggregate amount of such deductions is governed by certain percentage limitations. Corporations may deduct a maximum of ten percent of their taxable income. Individuals may deduct up to 50 percent of their adjusted gross income for contributions to churches, educational organizations, governmental units, and other defined organizations, but may deduct only 30 percent for contributions to other charities.

Contributors of capital gain property, such as art work, are limited to a 30 percent deduction for contributions to churches, schools, and so forth, but may deduct only 20 percent of contributions made to other charities. Under the alternative minimum tax provisions of IRC 55-59, appreciated property donated to charity is treated as a tax preference, with certain exceptions to encourage donation of art objects to museums and galleries by allowing collectors to deduct the fair market value, rather than basis, of their donations. The provision expired on July 1, 1992, but Congress may retroactively extend the provision.

Insurance Premiums

Shareholders in a corporate gallery or retail shop, regardless of whether it is a C or S corporation, may obtain some survivors' benefits by use of their stock interest through a contract known as a buy-sell agreement. In the event of the shareholder's death or disability, or, in most cases, his or her desire to sell out, this type of agreement essentially provides a mechanism for the purchase of a shareholder's stock by either the corporation or the other shareholders.

Insurance is frequently used to fund the death and disability portions of these agreements—the corporation agrees to purchase the shareholder's stock with the insurance proceeds in the event of the shareholder's death or disability. If the corporation owns the policy, it may deduct the cost of the premiums paid.

There are a variety of ways of structuring these arrangements, and you should consult a financial planner or insurance sales person, as well as your tax adviser and lawyer when developing these arrangements in order to determine which one will best serve your objectives. Also periodically review your plan with your attorney so that it reflects the constant changes in tax and business laws.

Taxable and Tax-Exempt Benefit Plans

Statutory Plans

Statutory, tax-exempt benefit plans are available for accident and health coverage, group-term life insurance, profit sharing, pension, and contributory savings plans, to name a few. Even though the myriad rules and regulations are tedious, the plans are worth consideration. If a plan conforms to the rules, employer contributions are immediately deductible as business expenses, but not taxable to the employees as income. Employees are taxed only when they receive payments from the plan. Even more important, in the case of some retirement plans, no tax is imposed on the investment growth of funds deposited in the plan.

For example, if your gallery or retail business is a C corporation, and the corporation's Board of Directors adopts a medical, dental, or vision plan, the corporation may purchase appropriate insurance or establish a reimbursement program. The corporation's expenses—insurance premiums or amounts reimbursed—will be paid with "pretax" dollars, and the employee will not be taxed on the benefits. These plans are not limited to corporate employers.

Statutory benefit plans can provide accident, medical, or group-term life insurance, educational assistance, legal services, or child care. Each is covered by separate rules and requirements that are extremely complex from a tax standpoint; retirement plans must also comply with the federal Employment Retirement Income Security Act (ERISA). But in order to be tax exempt, all plans must meet a common set of requirements, which prevent discrimination in favor of highly compensated employees:

- At least 90 percent of the employees who are not highly compensated must be eligible to participate in the plan. These employees must be entitled to at least 50 percent of the highest benefit provided to any highly compensated employee under this plan or any similar plan.

- At least 50 percent of the employees eligible to participate in the plan must be other than highly compensated employees.

- Eligibility requirements cannot be rigged to favor highly compensated employees.

A highly compensated employee is an employee who owns five percent of the business, or receives compensation in excess of $75,000 annually, or receives over $50,000 and is in the highest paid group of employees for the year, or is an officer and receives more than $45,000 in compensation annually.

Of course, if a small business had more highly compensated employees than other employees, a plan could not meet the 50 percent test, even if everyone received identical benefits. An alternative plan for eligibility will qualify a plan if the percentage of nonhighly compensated employees eligible for the plan equals or exceeds the percentage of highly compensated employees eligible for the same or all similar plans.

A statutory plan also must meet a benefits requirement so that the average benefit received by nonhighly compensated employees must equal or exceed 75 percent of the average benefits received by highly compensated employees under the same or similar plans.

In determining the required eligibility percentages, the following employees may be excluded: temporary and part-time employees, employees who are under 21 years old, employees covered by collective bargaining agreements (unions), employees who are nonresident aliens and who receive no U.S. taxable income, and employees who have been on the job less than one year (six months in the case of medical benefits).

Here are some sample guidelines for statutory plans:

Contributions by employers to health and accident plans are generally tax exempt only if they provide continuing extensions of coverage for various specified time periods. Amounts received to compensate an employee for loss of income due to illness or injury are taxable as income. When an employee receives payment for medical expenses, the amount received is not taxable income unless the employee is already receiving compensation from another source or takes an income tax deduction for the medical expenses. The employee is also not taxed on amounts received to compensate for injury due to permanent loss of use of a body part or function or permanent disfigurement.

If a plan provides assistance for child or other dependent care, the aggregate amount excluded from the employee's income cannot exceed $5,000 in the case of either an individual parent or a husband and wife together. If an employee receives $2,500 of tax-free child care assistance, the spouse is eligible to receive only an additional $2,500 in tax-free assistance.

1. An employer may provide up to $50,000 dollars of tax-free, group-term life insurance for each employee. Premiums on coverage exceeding $50,000 in face amount are taxable to employees, unless the employee contributes to the plan with his or her own taxable income.

2. An employee may receive up to $4,250 in tax-free educational assistance per year from a funded educational-assistance program.

Qualified Plans

Qualified plans include pensions, profit-sharing, and stock-bonus plans. Retirement benefits may also be provided under qualified plans.

Qualified plans must be separately funded and administered under rules designed to guarantee, to the extent possible, that retirement funds cannot be reached, tampered with, squandered, or mismanaged by the employer. There are also vesting requirements so that employees can rely on the plans without worrying about forfeiture due to excessively long employment period requirements.

Eligibility and benefit rules, similar to those for statutory plans, exist to assure nondiscrimination in qualified plans. To allow for different employer contribution amounts to various plans based upon an employee's value and years of service, there are special rules to prevent and remedy top-heavy plans in which accumulated contributions on behalf of highly compensated employees exceed those for other employees.

The rules for qualified pension, profit sharing, and stock bonus plans are too numerous to summarize. Maintenance of a qualified plan is impossible without specialized professional help—financial planners, business advisors, and skilled business attorneys.

Cafeteria Plans

Cafeteria plans have nothing to do with employee lunch rooms. Under a cafeteria plan, an employer may set up a "menu" whereby an employee is allotted a certain amount of benefit credit and can choose between various amounts and combinations of plans or the receipt of additional taxable income. The amounts allocable to elected benefit plans are not taxable to the employee. In this way, an employee can tailor a benefits program to best meet his or her individual circumstances. Fringe benefits and educational assistance plans may not be included in cafeteria plans.

Fringe Benefits

Certain fringe benefits may be provided tax free to employees, for example, employee discounts, subsidized cafeterias, parking facilities, on-site athletic facilities, etc. Generally, these benefits must be of no additional cost to the employer, or be worth so little that the administrative cost of keeping track of them exceeds the value of the benefit.

Shareholder employees of C corporations can take advantage of all of the above fringe benefits as employees. S corporation shareholders generally cannot avail themselves of certain fringe benefits, fully deductible health insurance at the corporate level, dependent care plans, or group term life plans.

Tax Shelters

Although they generate much interest, tax shelters do not ordinarily relieve a taxpayer of the obligation of paying tax; rather, they utilize loopholes in the tax law to postpone or defer tax liability. They accomplish this in one of two ways: (1) by accelerating deductions in the early years of investment, rather than matching deductions with the income as it is generated, and (2) by increasing the basis upon which the tax benefits are calculated without increasing the cash cost of the investment.

Although shelters may be very advantageous to the taxpayer, Congress and the IRS are extremely diligent in closing such loopholes as they are exploited, so you should update your benefit packages regularly.

One type of tax shelter available to gallery owners and crafts retailers involves an investment tax credit available under IRC 46 for qualified rehabilitation expenditures, such as restoring an historic structure. This is one of the few shelters that Congress appears to favor. It is a means by which the legislature can encourage rehabilitation activities it deems beneficial.

The amount of investment tax credit is 20 percent for certified historic structures and ten percent for other qualifying structures. The taxpayer deducts the tax credit directly from taxes owed. To qualify, most buildings must be nonresidential at the time rehabilitation begins; however, certified historic buildings can be either residential or nonresidential. The building also must have been placed in service before the beginning of the rehabilitation and it must have been substantially rehabilitated, with 50 percent or more of the existing external walls retained as external walls. Also, the taxpayer must elect to use a straight-line method of depreciation rather than accelerated methods. For certified historic structures, approval of the rehabilitation must be obtained from the Secretary of the Interior.

There may be other ways to structure tax shelters and to reduce one's tax liability. New schemes constantly are being devised by creative lawyers and accountants as the tax laws are continually changing. Plan your tax strategies carefully, and you can save significant amounts of money.

CHAPTER 21
Estate Planning

■ ALL GALLERY OWNERS AND CRAFTS retailers should give some thought to estate planning and take the time to execute a will. Without a will, there is simply no way to control the disposition of one's property after death. Sound estate planning may include transfers outside of the will, which will avoid the delays and expenses of probate, as well as certain types of trusts.

Successful estate planning is complex. Proper planning will require the assistance of a knowledgeable lawyer and perhaps also a life insurance agent, an accountant, or a bank trust officer, depending on the nature and size of the estate. This chapter is intended to introduce you to the basic principles of estate planning, alert you to potential problems, and prepare you to work with your estate planners.

The Will

A *will* is a legal instrument by which a person directs the distribution of property in his or her estate upon death. The maker of the will is called the *testator*. Gifts given by a will are referred to as *bequests* (personal property) or *devises* (real estate). The recipients of the bequests or devises are called *beneficiaries*.

Certain formalities are required by state law to create a valid will, and they vary from state to state. A few states also have special provisions known as community property laws, which would for example, characterize property acquired during marriage as owned by both spouses. About 30 states allow only formally witnessed wills, that is,

the instrument must be in writing and signed by the testator in the presence of two or more witnesses. The rest of the states allow either witnessed or unwitnessed wills. If a will is entirely handwritten by and signed by the testator, it is known as a holographic will.

A will is a unique document in two respects. First, if properly drafted it is ambulatory, meaning it can accommodate change—for example, apply to property acquired after the will is made. Second, a will is revocable, meaning that the testator has the power to change or cancel it before death. Even if a testator makes a valid agreement not to revoke the will, the power to revoke it remains, though liability for breach of contract could result.

Generally, courts do not consider a will to have been revoked unless it can be established that the testator either (1) performed a physical act of revocation, such as burning or tearing up a will, with intent to revoke it; or (2) executed a valid later will that revoked the previous will. Most state statutes also provide for automatic revocation of a will in whole or in part if the testator is subsequently divorced or married.

To change a will, the testator must execute a supplement, known as a *codicil*, which has the same formal requirements as those for creating a will. To the extent that the codicil contradicts the will, those contradicted parts of the will are revoked.

Payment of Testator's Debts

When the property owned by the testator at death is insufficient to satisfy all the bequests in the will after all debts and taxes have been paid, some or all of the bequests in the will must be reduced or even eliminated entirely. The process of reducing or eliminating bequests is known as abatement, and the priorities for reduction are set according to the category of each bequest. The legally significant categories of gifts are generally as follows:

- Specific bequests or devises, that is, gifts of identifiable items ("I give to X all the furniture in my home")

- Demonstrative bequests or devises, that is, gifts that are to be paid out of a specified source, unless that source contains insufficient funds, in which case the gifts will be paid out of the general assets ("I give to Y $1,000 to be paid from my shares of stock in ABC Corporation")

- General bequests, that is, gifts payable out of the general assets of an estate ("I give Z $1,000")

- Residuary bequests or devises, or gifts of whatever is left in the estate after all other gifts and expenses are satisfied ("I give the rest, residue and remainder of my estate, to Z")

The property not governed by a will is called intestate property, and is usually the first to be taken to satisfy claims against the estate. If the will contains a valid residuary clause, there will be no such property. In this case, residuary bequests are the first taken. If more money is needed, general bequests will be taken, and lastly, specific and demonstrative bequests will be taken together in proportion to their value. Some states provide that all gifts, regardless of type, abate proportionately.

Disposition of Property Not Willed

If the testator acquires more property after signing the will but before death, the disposition of such property will also be governed by the will. If such property falls within the description of an existing category in the will ("I give all my stock to X; I give all my real estate to Y"), it will pass along with all similar property. If it does not, and the will contains a valid residuary clause, the property will go to the residuary legatees. If there is no such clause, this property will pass outside the will to the persons specified in the state's law of *intestate* succession.

When a person dies without leaving a valid will, the person is said to have died intestate. The property of a person who dies intestate is distributed according to the state law of intestate succession, which specifies who is entitled to what parts of the estate. An intestate's surviving spouse will always receive a share, generally at least one third of the estate. An intestate's surviving children likewise always get a share. If some of the children do not survive the intestate, the grandchildren of the intestate may be entitled to a share by representation.

Representation is a legal principle that specifies if an heir does not survive the intestate, but has a child who does survive, that child will represent the nonsurviving heir and receive that parent's share in the estate.

If there are no direct descendants surviving, the intestate's surviving spouse will take the entire estate or share it with the intestate's parents. If there is neither a surviving spouse nor any surviving direct descendant of the intestate, the estate will be distributed to the intestate's parents, or if the parents are not surviving, to the intestate's siblings by representation. If there are no surviving persons in any of these categories, the estate will go to surviving grandparents and their direct descendants. In this way the family tree is constantly expanded in search of surviving relatives. The laws of intestate succession make no provision for friends, in-laws, or stepchildren. If none of the persons specified in the law of intestate succession survive the testator, the intestate's property ultimately goes to the state. This reversion of property to the state in the absence of legal heirs is known as *escheat*.

State law will often provide a testator's surviving spouse with certain benefits from the estate even if the spouse is left out of the testator's will. Historically, these benefits were known as *dower*, in the case of a surviving wife, or *curtesy*, in the case of a surviving husband. The historical concepts of dower and curtesy are in large part a result of the law's traditional recognition of an absolute duty on the part of the husband to provide for the wife. Modern laws are perhaps better justified by the notion that most property in a marriage should be shared because the financial success of either partner is due to the efforts of both. In place of the old dower and curtesy, modern statutes give the surviving spouse the right to elect against the will, and thereby receive a share equal to at least one fourth of the estate. Here again, state laws vary—in some states, the surviving spouse's elective share is one third.

Advantages to Having a Will

A will affords one the opportunity to directly distribute one's property and to give gifts conditionally, when that is preferred. For example, if an individual wishes to donate certain property to a specific charity, but only if certain conditions are adhered to, a will can make such conditions a prerequisite to the donation.

A will permits the testator to nominate an *executor*—called a personal representative in some states—to watch over the estate. If no executor is named in the will, the court will appoint one. If the testator has an unusual type of property, such as antiques, art, or publishable manuscripts, it is a good idea to appoint joint executors, one with financial expertise and the other with expertise in valuation of antiques, in art, or in publishing.

Some provision should be made in the will for resolving any deadlock between joint executors. For example, a neutral third party might be appointed as an arbitrator, directed to resolve any impasses after hearing both sides. It is also advisable to define the scope of the executor's power by detailed instructions.

A lawyer's help will be necessary to set forth all of these important considerations in legally enforceable, unambiguous terms. It is essential in a will to avoid careless language that might be subject to attack by survivors who are unhappy with the will's provisions. A lawyer's help is also crucial to avoid making bequests that are not legally enforceable because they are contrary to public policy (e.g., a bequest that inhibits legal marriage or states that if one gets married the bequest will fail).

In addition to giving the testator significant posthumous control over division of property, a carefully drafted will can greatly reduce the overall amount of estate tax paid at death.

The taxing structures I'll discuss here relate to federal estate taxation. State estate taxes often contain similar provisions, but consult your lawyer regarding the specifics of your state's laws.

The Gross Estate

The first step in evaluating an estate for tax purposes is to determine the so-called gross estate. The gross estate includes all property over which the deceased had significant control at the time of death, for example, certain life insurance proceeds and annuities, jointly held interests, revocable transfers, and interests in business.

Under current tax laws, the executor of an estate may elect to value the property in the estate either as of the date of death or as of a date six months after death. The estate property must be valued in its entirety at the chosen time. If the executor elects to value the estate six months after death, however, and certain pieces of property are distributed or sold before then, that property will be valued as of the date of distribution or sale.

Fair market value is defined as the price at which property would change hands between a willing buyer and a willing seller, when both buyer and seller have reasonable knowledge of all relevant facts. Such a determination is often very difficult to make, especially when items such as artwork are involved. Although the initial determination of fair market value is generally made by the executor when the estate tax return is filed, the Internal Revenue Service may disagree with the executor's valuation and assign assets a much higher fair market value. For example, in 1979 the IRS claimed that Jacqueline Susann's diary had an estate tax value of $3,800,000 as a literary property. The diary, which neither Susann nor her executor had considered particularly valuable, had been destroyed by the executor pursuant to Susann's directions.

When an executor and the Internal Revenue Service disagree as to valuation, the court will decide the matter. In most cases, the burden will be on the taxpayer to prove the value of the asset. Thus, expert testimony and evidence of the sale of the same or similar properties will be helpful, as in cases involving original manuscripts and drawings. In general, courts are reluctant to determine valuation by formula.

Generally, estate taxes must be paid when the estate tax return is filed (within nine months of the date of death), although arrangements may be made to spread payments out over a number of years if necessary. It is not uncommon for executors to be forced to sell properties for less than full value in order to pay taxes. This can be avoided by obtaining insurance policies, the proceeds of which can be set up in a trust (see chapter 17).

The Taxable Estate

After determining the gross estate, the second step in evaluating an estate for tax purposes is figuring the taxable estate. The taxable estate is the basis upon which the owed tax is computed.

The law allows a number of deductions from the gross estate in determining the amount of the taxable estate. Typical deductions include funeral expenses, certain estate administration expenses, debts and enforceable claims against the estate, mortgages and liens, and, perhaps most significant, the marital deduction and the charitable deduction.

The marital deduction allows the total value of any interest in property that passes from the decedent to the surviving spouse to be subtracted from the value of the gross estate. The government will eventually get its tax on this property and its appreciated value when that spouse dies, but only to the extent such interest is included in the spouse's gross estate. This deduction may occur even in the absence of the will's specifically making a gift to the surviving spouse; state law generally provides that the spouse is entitled to at least one fourth of the overall estate, regardless of the provisions of the will.

The charitable deduction refers to the deduction allowed upon the transfer of property from an estate to a recognized charity. Because the definition of a charity for tax purposes is quite technical, it is advisable to insert a clause in the will providing that if the institution specified to receive the donation does not qualify for the charitable deduction, the bequest shall go to a substitute qualified institution at the choice of the executor.

Once the deductions are computed, the taxable estate is taxed at the rate specified by the Unified Estate and Gift Tax Schedule. The unified tax imposes the same rate of tax on gifts made by a will as on gifts made during life. It is a progressive tax, meaning the percentage paid in taxes increases with the amount of property involved. The rates rise significantly for larger estates, for example, from 18% where the cumulative total of taxable estate and taxable gifts is under $10,000, to 55% where the cumulative total is over $3,000,000. Tax credits are provided by year according to the tax schedule. Federal estate tax is also reduced by state death tax credit or actual state death tax, whichever is less. Gift and estate tax credits result in a $600,000 exemption, which is available to every estate. This exemption, combined with the unlimited marital deduction, allows most estates to escape estate taxes altogether. In estates in excess of $10,000,000, the unified tax credit begins to decline.

Distributing Property Outside the Will

Property can be distributed outside of the will by making *inter vivos* gifts (during the giver's lifetime) either by giving the gift outright or by placing the property in trust. The main advantage to distributing property outside of the will is that the property escapes the delays and expense of probate, which is the court procedure by which a will is validated and administered. There used to be significant tax advantages to making *inter vivos,* or living, gifts rather than gifts by will, but because the estate and gift tax rates are now unified, there are only a few remaining tax advantages.

One advantage is that if the *inter vivos* gift appreciates in value between the time the gift is made and death, the appreciated value will not be taxed. If the gift were made by will, the added value would be taxable because the gift would be valued as of the date of death (or six months after). This value difference can represent significant tax savings for the heirs of someone whose business suddenly becomes successful and rapidly increases in value.

The other advantage to making an *inter vivos* gift is the yearly exclusion of $10,000 per recipient. For example, if $15,000 worth of gifts were given to an individual in one year, only $5,000 worth of gifts would be taxable to the donor (who is responsible for the gift tax). A married couple can combine their gifts and claim a yearly exclusion of $20,000 per recipient.

Gifts made within three years of death used to be included in the gross estate, in accordance with the theory that these gifts were made in contemplation of death. Recent amendments to the tax laws, however, have done away with the three-year rule for most purposes. The three-year rule is still applicable to gifts of life insurance, to certain transfers involving stock redemptions or tax liens, and to certain complex valuation schemes.

Gift tax returns must be filed by the donor for any year in which gifts made to any one donee exceeded $10,000. It's not necessary to file a return if gifts to any one donee amount to less than $10,000, however, if it's possible that the valuation of the gifts might be questioned by the IRS, it may be a good idea to file a return anyway. Filing the return starts the three-year statute of limitations period. Once the statute of limitations period has expired, the IRS is barred from filing suit for unpaid taxes or for tax deficiencies due to higher government valuations of the gifts. If a taxpayer omits includable gifts amounting to more than 25% of the total amount of gifts stated in the return, the statute of limitations is extended to six years. There is no statute of limitations for fraudulent returns filed with the intent to evade tax.

In order to qualify as an *inter vivos* gift for tax purposes, a gift must be complete and final. Control is an important issue. If a giver retains the right to revoke a gift (not made in trust), the gift may be found to be testamentary in nature, that is, created by the will, even if the right to revoke was never exercised, and therefore is not *inter vivos.* The gift must also be delivered. An actual, physical delivery is best, but a symbolic delivery may suffice if there is strong evidence of intent to make an irrevocable gift—for example, the donor gives the gift's recipient the only key to the safe containing the gift.

Another common way to transfer property outside the will is to place the property in a *trust* that is created prior to death. A trust is simply a legal arrangement by which one person holds certain property for the benefit of one or more others. The person holding the property is the *trustee;* those for whose benefit it is held are the *beneficiaries.*

To create a valid trust, the giver must identify the trust property; make a declaration of intent to create the trust; transfer property to the trust; and name identifiable beneficiaries. If no trustee is named, a court will appoint one. The *settlor,* or creator of the trust, may also be designated as trustee, in which case segregation of the trust property in a separate account or trust satisfies the delivery requirement.

Trusts can be created by will, but these testamentary trust properties will be probated along with the rest of the will. To avoid probate, the settlor must create a valid *inter vivos* trust. Generally, in order to qualify as an *inter vivos* trust, a valid interest in property must be transferred before the death of the creator of the trust. If the settlor fails to name a beneficiary for the trust or make delivery of the property to the trustee before death, the trust will likely be termed testamentary—that is, to be disposed of after death. Such a trust will be deemed invalid unless the formalities required for creating a will were complied with.

A trust will not be termed testamentary simply because the settlor retained significant control over the trust, such as the power to revoke or modify the trust. For example, when a person makes a deposit in a savings account in his or her own name as trustee for another, and reserves the power to withdraw the money or revoke the trust, the trust will be enforceable by the beneficiary upon the death of the depositor, providing the depositor has not in fact revoked the trust. Many states allow the same type of arrangement in authorizing joint bank accounts with rights of survivorship as valid will substitutes.

Property transferred under one of these arrangements is thus passed outside the will and need not go through probate. However, even though such an arrangement escapes probate, the trust property will probably be considered part of the gross estate for tax purposes because the settlor retained significant control. In addition, if the deceased settlor created a revocable trust for the purpose of decreasing the share of a surviving spouse, in some states the trust will be declared illusory—in effect invalid. The surviving spouse is then granted the legal share not only from the probated estate but from the revocable trust.

Life insurance trusts can be used for paying estate taxes. The proceeds will not be taxed if the life insurance trust is irrevocable and the beneficiary is someone other than the estate, such as a friend or relative acting in an individual capacity (not a representative or agent of a corporation) or the business. This is especially important for entrepreneurs, because, without a life insurance trust, their survivors might be forced to sell estate assets for less than their real value in order to pay estate taxes.

CHAPTER 22

How to Find a Lawyer and an Accountant

■ MOST GALLERY OWNERS and crafts retailers expect to seek the advice of a lawyer only occasionally for counseling on important matters, such as whether or not to incorporate or what to do when they are sued. If this is your concept of the attorney's role in your business, I recommend you reevaluate it. Most small galleries and crafts retailers would operate more efficiently and more profitably in the long run if they had a relationship with a business attorney similar to that between a family doctor and his patient—that is, an ongoing relationship that allows the attorney to get to know the business well enough to engage in preventive legal counseling and assist in planning. This type of relationship with your attorney will make it possible to avoid problems before they occur.

If your business is small or undercapitalized, you're most likely anxious to keep operating costs down. You probably do not relish the idea of paying an attorney to get to know your business if you are not involved in an immediate crisis. However, it's a good bet that a conversation with a competent business lawyer right now will raise issues vital to the future of your gallery. There is good reason why large, successful businesses employ one or more attorneys full time as in-house counsel. Ready access to legal advice is something you should not deny your business at any time, for any reason.

An attorney experienced in representing art galleries or crafts retailers can give you important information regarding the risks unique to your business. Furthermore, a lawyer can advise you regarding your rights and obligations in your rela-

tionship with present and future employees; the rules that apply in your state regarding the hiring and firing of employees; permissible collection practices; and so forth, as I've mentioned throughout this book. Ignorance of these issues and violation of the rules can result in financially devastating lawsuits and, in some situations, even criminal penalties. Each state has its own laws covering certain business practices, and a competent art or crafts lawyer is your best source of information on many state laws that will effect the running of your business.

What's really behind all the hoopla about preventive legal counseling? Are we lawyers simply seeking more work? Admittedly, as business people, lawyers want business. But what you should consider is this economic reality: Most legal problems cost more to solve or defend after they arise than it would have cost to prevent their occurrence in the first place. Litigation is notoriously inefficient and expensive. You do not want to sue or be sued if you can help it. The expense is shocking; for instance, it can cost more than $100 per day simply to use a courtroom for trial. Pretrial procedures run into the thousands of dollars for most cases. The cost of defending a case filed against you or your business is something you have no choice but to incur, unless you choose to default, which is almost never advisable.

The lawyer who will be most valuable to your young business will likely not be a Raymond Burr or Robert Redford character, but rather a meticulous person who does most of his or her work in an office, reviewing your business forms, your employee contracts, or your corporate bylaws. This person should have a good reputation in the legal community, as well as in the business community.

One of the first items you should discuss with your lawyer is the fee structure. You are entitled to an estimate, but unless you enter into an agreement to the contrary with the attorney, the estimate is just that. Business lawyers generally charge by the hour, though you may be quoted a flat rate for a specific service, such as incorporation or registering your trademark. You will probably pay over $100 per hour for an attorney's services, but if the firm has a good reputation, it employs a well-trained professional staff that can reduce the total amount of time required.

Finding a Lawyer

If you do not know any attorneys, ask other gallery owners or craft retailers whether or not they know any good ones. You want either a lawyer who specializes in art law, or a general practitioner who has many happy gallery owners or craft retailers as clients.

It is a good idea to hire a specialist or a firm with a number of specialists. Although it's true that you may pay more per hour for the expert, you will not have to fund his or her learning time, and experience is valuable. In this regard, keep in mind that it is uncommon for a lawyer to specialize in business practice and also handle criminal matters. Thus, if you are faced with a criminal prosecution for the death of an employee, you should be searching for an experienced criminal defense lawyer.

Finding the lawyer who is right for you is like finding the right doctor—you may have to shop around a bit. Your city, county, and state bar associations may have helpful referral services. A good tip is to find out who is in the art law section of the state or county bar association, if it has one, or who has served on special bar committees dealing with art law reform. Or check with the law school in your area to find out who teaches a course in the field. You can also consult the Martindale-Hubbell Law Directory in your county law library. The mere fact that an attorney's name does not appear in the book should not be given too much weight, however, because there's a charge for being included, and some lawyers may have chosen not to pay for the listing.

It also may be useful to find out whether any articles covering the area of law you are concerned with have been published in scholarly journals, continuing legal education publications, or trade publications such as *NICHE Magazine* or *The Crafts Report,* and whether the author is available to assist you.

After you have compiled a list of attorneys who might suit your needs, it is appropriate for you to talk with them for a short period of time to determine whether or not you would be comfortable working with them. Don't be afraid to ask about their background and experience, and whether or not they feel they can help you with your specific concerns. Some lawyers will bill you for the initial consultation, so be sure to ask about this when making your appointment.

Once you have completed the interview process, select the person who appears to best satisfy your needs. The rest is up to you. Contact your lawyer whenever you believe a legal question has arisen. Your attorney should help you identify those questions that require legal action or advice and those that require business advice. Generally, lawyers will deal only with legal issues, although they may help you to evaluate business problems. You should be aware that you are likely to be charged for all consultations, even though they may only be brief telephone calls, but the cost is well worth the investment.

I encourage my clients to call me at the office during the day or at home in the evening. Some lawyers, however, may resent having their personal time invaded. Some, in fact, do not list their home telephone numbers. You should learn your attorney's preference early on.

You should feel comfortable confiding in your attorney. The attorney-client relationship is such that this person will not disclose your confidential communications; in fact, a violation of this rule, depending on the circumstances, can be considered an ethical breach that could subject the attorney to professional sanctions.

Take the time to develop a good working relationship with your attorney. It may well prove to be one of your more valuable business assets.

Finding an Accountant

You'll also need the services of a competent accountant to aid with structuring your business, tax planning, and filing periodic and annual tax returns. The task of finding a CPA with whom your business is compatible is similar to the task of finding an attorney. You should ask around and learn which accountants are servicing galleries or shops similar to yours. State or local professional accounting associations may also provide a referral service or point you to a directory of accountants in your region. Interview prospective accountants to determine whether or not you feel you can work with them comfortably and effectively and whether you feel their skills are compatible with your business needs.

Like your attorney, your accountant can provide valuable assistance in planning the future of your business. In both cases, it is important to work with professionals you trust and with whom you are able to relate on a professional level.

Appendices

appendices

APPENDIX A

BILL OF SALE

Terms Net	Cash Sale ☐	Credit Card #_____ Exp. _____	
Ship to:	_____	Bill to: _____	Date
	_____	_____	Via

Item No.	Description: Medium, Title, Dimensions (Height x Width)	Price

All sales subject to terms and conditions on reverse of this invoice.

Received in good condition:	Net	$
	Sales Tax	$
_____ Buyer's Signature Date	Total	$

(Bill of Sale/Reverse Side)

Terms and Conditions of Sale

Payment for all works herein shall be in United States currency, net on presentation of this invoice. Works may also be charged on valid credit accounts.

Unless otherwise specifically indicated, all works herein are originals, executed by the artist and are certified to be free from all defects due to faulty craftsmanship or faulty materials for a period of twelve months from the date of sale. If flaws should occur during this period and appear to be due to these causes, said works shall be subject to repair or replacement, at the option of the Seller. Buyer is cautioned, however, that the Seller cannot be responsible for fading, cracking, and other damage to these works caused by improvident exposure to sunlight and weather.

The Buyer may return any work acquired herein for full credit against the purchase of any other works available at that time, provided only that said work shall be returned in good condition and within 30 days from the date hereof.

All shipments are fully insured by the Seller against damage or loss. If works are not received in good condition please notify the Seller at once.

All shipments are F.O.B. the gallery and will be transferred via freight collect, unless prepaid by the Buyer. Crating methods and charges are per art object freight company standard procedures and rates.

APPENDIX B–1

Contract No. _____

Code No. _____

Customer No. _____

Date _____

O.A.I. Expires _____

RENTAL AGREEMENT

The undersigned acknowledges receipt of a copy of this agreement and agrees to rent the work of art listed below from the _____ **Gallery** according to the terms of this agreement set out below:

Title _____ Medium _____

Artist _____ Price _____

Condition _____

Simultaneously herewith, the undersigned has paid to the _____ **Gallery** $_____, the rental fee for the above-described work, plus a transaction fee of $_____, for a total of $_____. It is understood that the rental period may be renewed for one consecutive three-month period by payment to the Gallery, prior to the expiration of the original term of the lease, the total fee of $____. If the renter exercises the option to rent for an additional three-month period, the provisions of this agreement shall remain in effect. The renter shall return the artwork to the gallery at the end of the three-month period or, if the contract is renewed, at the end of the three-month renewal period. It is understood that the rental fees for not more than two consecutive three-month periods may be applied to the purchase price of the above-described work of art. THE TRANSACTION FEES DO NOT APPLY TO THE PURCHASE PRICE.

The renter acknowledges receipt of the article in good condition unless otherwise indicated on this agreement, and agrees to return it in the same condition at the expiration of this agreement or extension hereof. The renter shall not clean or repair the article or remove it from its frame or base or in any other way alter it. Acceptance by the _____ **Gallery** of the return of the article shall not be construed as a waiver of any claim it may have for damage to the article prior to the return thereof even though works are insured by the _____ **Gallery**.

The renter agrees not to sketch, photograph, reproduce or otherwise use the article for advertising or commercial purposes, or permit any other person to do so without written permission of the artist. The renter shall not sublease the art work or assign this agreement. It is further understood that this art work will be kept at the address shown below.

It is understood that transportation of the art work to and from the Gallery is the responsibility of the renter, and that suitable precautions shall be observed in transit. If the renter fails to return the article when due, it is understood that a charge of 50 cents will be made for each day of Gallery operation that this work is overdue, for 12 working days, with the charge to be increased to $5.00 per day thereafter until returned, plus any cost or expense incurred by the Gallery in recovering possession thereof. The Gallery or its agents are expressly authorized to enter the premises of the renter and to remove the article without penalty or liability for trespass at any time after expiration of this agreement or extension hereof.

The renter agrees to pay the Gallery the reasonable attorneys' fees and other costs incurred by the Gallery in enforcing this agreement, whether or not a legal proceeding is commenced, including fees incurred before a legal proceeding, in a legal proceeding, or on appeal.

Original expiration date _____ Signed _____

Bill _____ Paid _____ Name _____

RENEWAL _____ Address _____

Renewal expiration date _____ _____

City _____

RETURNED _____ State _____ ZIP _____

Signed _____ Telephone No. _____
(_____ **Gallery** Representative)

APPENDIX B–2
(Modified by Author)

Contract No. _____

Code No. _____

Customer Account No. _____

Date _____

PURCHASE CONTRACT

I agree to purchase the work of art described below from the _____ **Gallery**, according to the terms set forth below:

Title _____ Artist _____

1. Cash Price .... $ _____

2. (Less:) A. Applicable Rental Previously Paid ....$ _____
   B. Cash Down Payment ....$ _____
   C. Total Down Payment .... $ _____

3. Unpaid Balance of Cash Price (Amount Financed) .... $ _____

4. **FINANCE CHARGE** .... $ ____-0-

5. Total of Payments (3 +4) .... $ _____

6. Deferred Payment Price (1 + 4) .... $ _____

7. **ANNUAL PERCENTAGE RATE** .... $ ____-0-

8. $1.00 per payment handling charge due with each monthly payment.

9. The Total of Payments is payable in ____ consecutive installments of $ _____ each on the _____ day of each month, commencing _____, and continuing until paid in full.

10. **Default Charges and Acceleration**

    A. **Costs and Attorney's Fees.** If it becomes necessary for you to incur costs in collecting this account, I will pay all such costs, including reasonable attorney's fees (for an attorney not your salaried employee), and, if suit or action is instituted to collect the account, I will pay such reasonable attorney fees both at trial and on appeal.

    B. **Acceleration.** If I fail to make any payment within 30 days of the date on which it is due, you may declare due the entire unpaid balance under this agreement.

11. **Prepayment.** I may prepay all amounts due at any time without penalty.

12. **Security.** To secure my obligations, I grant you a purchase money security interest under ___ [state] Uniform Commercial Code in the property sold under this agreement. You will have all of the rights of a secured party under the ____[state] Uniform Commercial Code, including the right of peaceable repossession of the property in the event of a default. I agree that I will make the property available to you at a place that you reasonably may specify upon default and that copies of this agreement may be filed as a financing statement.

I acknowledge receipt of a copy of this agreement, completely filled out, and agree to its terms.

Signed _____

Accepted: Name _____

_____ Address _____
(_____ **Gallery** Representative)

APPENDIX B-3

Contract No. _____

Code No. _____

PURCHASE CONTRACT PAYMENT SCHEDULE

Unpaid balance of Cash Price ....$ _____

No.	Date Received	Amount	Balance Due
(1)	_____	$ _____	$ _____
(2)	_____	$ _____	$ _____
(3)	_____	$ _____	$ _____
(4)	_____	$ _____	$ _____
(5)	_____	$ _____	$ _____
(6)	_____	$ _____	$ _____
(7)	_____	$ _____	$ _____
(8)	_____	$ _____	$ _____
(9)	_____	$ _____	$ _____
(10)	_____	$ _____	$ _____
(11)	_____	$ _____	$ _____
(12)	_____	$ _____	$ _____
(13)	_____	$ _____	$ _____
(14)	_____	$ _____	$ _____
(15)	_____	$ _____	$ _____
(16)	_____	$ _____	$ _____
(17)	_____	$ _____	$ _____
(18)	_____	$ _____	$ _____
(19)	_____	$ _____	$ _____
(20)	_____	$ _____	$ _____

APPENDIX C

ARTIST-GALLERY CONSIGNMENT STATUTES

Alaska Stat. §§ 45.65.200 – .550 (1991)

Ariz. Rev. Stat. Ann. §§ 44–1771 – 1778 (1987 & Supp. 1990)

Ark. Stat. Ann. §§ 4–73–201 – 296 (1987)

Cal. Civ. Code §§ 1738 – 1738.6 (West 1985)

Colo. Rev. Stat. §§ 6–15–101 – 104 (1989)

Conn. Gen. Stat. §§ 42–116k – m (West 1987)

D.C. Code Ann. §§ 28:9–14 (1990)

Fla. Stat. Ann. §§ 686.501 – .506 (West 1990)

Idaho Code §§ 28–11–101 – 106 (1991)

Ill. Rev. Stat. ch. 121½, para. 1400 – 1408 (Smith–Hurd 1989)

Iowa Code Ann. §§ 556D.1 – 556D.5 (West Supp. 1991)

Ky. Rev. Stat. Ann. §§ 365.850 – .875 (Michie Replacement 1987)

Md. Com. Law Code Ann. §§ 11–8A–0 – 04 (Michie Replacement 1990)

Mass. Gen. Laws Ann. ch. 104A, §§ 1 – 6 (West 1984)

Mich. Stat. Ann. §§ 19.410(1) – (5) (Callaghan 1990)

Minn. Stat. Ann. §§ 324.01 – .05 (West 1991)

Mo. Ann. Stat. §§ 407.901 – .910 (Vernon 1990)

Mont. Code Ann. §§ 22–2–501 – 505 (1991)

N.H. Rev. Stat. Ann. §§ 352:3 – 352:12 (1990)

N.J. Stat. Ann. §§ 12A:2–329 – 336 (West Supp. 1991)

N.M. Stat. Ann. §§ 56–11–1 – 3 (1986)

N.Y. Arts & Cult. Aff. Law §§ 12.01 – .03 (McKinney Supp. 1991)

N.C. Gen. Stat. § 25C–2 (1989)

Ohio Rev. Code Ann. §§ 1339.71 – .78 (Baldwin 1989)

Or. Rev. Stat. §§ 359.200 – .255 (1989)

Pa. Stat. Ann. tit. 73, §§ 2121 – 2139 (Purdon Supp. 1991)

Tenn. Code Ann. §§ 47–25–1001 – 1007 (1980)

Tex. Rev. Civ. Stat. Ann. Art. 9018 (West Supp. 1991)

Wash. Rev. Code Ann. §§ 18.110.010 – .905 (1989)

Wis. Stat. Ann. §§ 129.01 – .08 (West 1989)

APPENDIX D

MODEL CONSIGNMENT AGREEMENT

*Model Consignment Agreement**

THIS AGREEMENT made and entered into this _____ day of
_____, 19___, and by and between Artist ("Artist") and Art
Gallery ("Gallery");

Witnesseth:

WHEREAS, Gallery is engaged in the business of the sale of works of art; and

WHEREAS, Artist has created, expended time and labor on, and does rightfully own
and possess certain works of art, more fully described in Exhibit A hereto, and desires to sell
the same;

NOW, THEREFORE, in consideration of value hereby acknowledged as received,
each party agrees as follows:

1. Covenants and Promises of Gallery

Gallery hereby covenants, promises, represents, agrees and acknowledges as follows:

(a)   Receipt on consignment of _____ (amount) artworks, as
described in Exhibit hereto:

(b)   To make reasonable and bona fide efforts to sell each said art work and, in any
event, at a price not less than that listed in Exhibit B hereto unless specifically
authorized by Artist, and, to that end, to display (within _____ weeks after receipt
of said artworks), _____ or more of said works and, continuously thereafter, a
combination of said works in that number (or more, as may subsequently be agreed
upon and set forth as Exhibit C to this Agreement) for a period of _____ weeks;

(c)   To exercise all due and reasonable care in the handling, display, storage, and
temporary delivery to other persons of said artworks until returned to the possession of
Artist;

(d)   To deliver to Artists on or before the 15th day of each month during the
effectiveness of this contract, a full and complete statement of inventory and account
for the preceding calendar month ("Statement") in approximately the form of Exhibit
___ hereto, which shall set forth the following:

(i)   the particular artwork(s) sold:

(ii) the date of such sale(s) and amount(s) and terms thereof (whether cash, barter, exchange, credit, partial payment, or other); and

(iii) the particularly–described location of all unsold artworks; and whether, if in the possession of Gallery, said unsold artworks are, at the time of said report, currently displayed (and for how long displayed) or not displayed.

Gallery hereby represents that said Statements shall be accurate and complete in all respects.

(e) In the event of sale of said consigned artworks, to remit to Artist within a reasonable time (or _____ days) after date of sale, together with a true copy of a bill of sale for each artwork or group of artworks sold (though the name of the purchaser may be omitted), _____ percentage of the consideration actually received before appropriate state sales tax; or, if the transaction were in the nature in whole or in part of an exchange, then the fair market value equivalent thereof;

PROVIDED, that, in the case of payment at time of sale of less than the full purchase price, the above percentage of the amount actually received by Gallery shall be delivered to Artist within seven (7) days after receipt thereof, as shall in like manner the same percentage of subsequent payments to Gallery;

(f) To return to Artist, within ____ days after receipt of a written demand therefor, all artworks consigned under this Agreement to Gallery and remaining unsold at time of said receipt;

(g) To refrain from seeking, in any way, to restrain Artist in the sale of any artworks other than consistently with this Agreement;

[If Paragraph 2(c) below is included, then]

[PROVIDED, that, in return for the promise of Artist as set forth in paragraph 2(c) hereof, Gallery will remit an additional ___% of the consideration received from any sale covered by this Agreement over and above that percentage provided in paragraph 1(e) hereof and such additional percentage shall be paid to Artist in the same manner and at the same time as the regular percentage provided in paragraph 1(d) hereof.]

(h) If Gallery should desire to enter any of the artworks covered by this Agreement in any art show in which awards are made, to obtain the written signature of Artist on any entry form used for the purpose or, in the event that there is no entry form, to obtain a written consent of Artist prior to entry in any such art show;

2. Covenants and Promises of Artist

Artist covenants, promises, represents, agrees and acknowledges as follows:

(a)   That Gallery is authorized during a period of ____ days (months) to deliver title to artworks covered by this Agreement to purchasers and to collect therefor a price no less than the minimum price set forth for that work or works in Exhibit ___;

(b)   That Gallery shall deliver to Artist a true copy of the bill of sale given the purchaser; and

(c)   That Gallery, after withholding from the purchase price such sum as is required by law for sales tax, and also, as Gallery's commission, a sum equal to _____% of the selling price, shall remit the balance received to Artist within a reasonable time (_____ days);

[Optional]

[(d)   That Artist will not, during the effectiveness of this Agreement, make any agreements, conditional or otherwise, to sell or to transfer at any time, the artwork contained in Exhibit ___ to this Agreement without the written consent of Gallery.]

(e)   Except as hereinafter provided, that Artist may, without consent of Gallery, sell or seek to sell any artworks not consigned under this Agreement and produced by Artist;

PROVIDED,

(i)   That with respect to artworks similar to the type and nature of those consigned under this Agreement, Artist shall not sell or seek to sell such artworks within a ____ mile radius of Gallery and within either a six- (6) month period commencing with the display, as provided in paragraph 1(a) of this Agreement, or within three (3) months after termination of this Agreement, whichever shall come first;

(ii)   That anything to the contrary notwithstanding, subparagraph 2(c)(i) [*sic*] above shall not apply to sales or selling efforts directed to any persons engaged in the business of wholesale or retail sales of such works;

(iii)   That subparagraph 2(c)(i) [*sic*] to the contrary notwithstanding, Artist may make sales within the area of the above radius without first securing permission of Gallery, on condition that of such sales occurring within the first six (6) months after initial display of at least three (3) consigned works by Gallery or, if this Agreement is for purposes of Gallery presenting a "one-man show" of Artist's works, within twelve (12) months after such initial display, Artist shall remit to Gallery _____ percent of the consideration before appropriate state sales tax, together with a true copy of the bill of sale for each artwork within seven (7) days after the transaction; and

(iv) That, in the case of payment at the time of sale of less than full purchase price, the above percentage of the amount actually received by Gallery, together with said true copy of the bill of sale, shall be delivered to Artist within seven (7) days after receipt thereof, and the same percentage of subsequent payments to Gallery within seven (7) days after receipt thereof;

(f) That Gallery may deliver any of the artworks consigned under this Agreement to prospective purchasers thereof for display for a reasonable period of time not to exceed _____ weeks in their residence, place of business, or other appropriate location; and

(g) To inform Gallery at all times during the effectiveness of this Agreement of any change in his present address from that entered in paragraph 8 of this Agreement.

3. Term of Effectiveness

Unless terminated by Gallery or Artist as otherwise provided, this Agreement shall continue in force and effect from the date hereunder until _____, 19_____, and thereafter from month to month until terminated by written notice given not less than ___ days prior to said termination date, or to the end of any month thereafter.

4. Termination

Except as hereinafter provided, this Agreement may be regarded by either party at its option as terminated and as of no further force and effect in the event of breach by the other party of any covenant, promise, representation or agreement made here:

PROVIDED,

(a) That, in the event of termination by Artist pursuant solely to paragraph 1(f) hereof and for no other cause, the provisions of paragraph 2(e) hereof shall continue in effect, unless expressly waived by Gallery;

(b) That, if Artist fails to comply with paragraph 2(g) hereof, any termination of this Agreement by Gallery shall be governed by the provisions of paragraph 5 hereof;

In addition, this Agreement shall terminate upon the death, involuntary bankruptcy, or dissolution of either party.

Upon termination, except when based on Artist's breach of paragraph 2(g) hereof, all works shall be returned to Artist or his successors or survivors, as provided in paragraph 1(f) hereof.

5. Termination by Gallery for Failure of Artist to Comply with Paragraph 2(e) of this Agreement

(a)   In the event that Artist fails to comply with paragraph 29(e) of this Agreement, Gallery may terminate this Agreement by sending by certified mail, return receipt requested, two (2) notices of termination, not less than one (1) week apart, to the last address furnished Gallery by Artist. Artist must pick up the artworks consigned under this Agreement and remaining in Gallery's possession from Gallery within thirty (30) days of the postmark date of second letter of termination, or Gallery may charge Artist for storage costs for [said works] at the rate of _____ Dollars per month, beginning thirty (30) days after the postmark date of said second letter of termination;

(b)   If, thirty (30) days after the postmark date of said second letter of termination, there are funds accruing to Artist's benefit by virtue of [the rental of said works] and Artist has failed to pick up said works, it is agreed that Gallery may use said funds in payment of storage costs as they become due;

(c)   If, at any time, storage charges equal or exceed the minimum selling price of the artwork set forth in Exhibit ___, as stated above, Artist agrees that title to said artwork shall pass to Gallery in satisfaction of and payment for said storage charges; and

(d)   Notwithstanding paragraph 5(c) hereof, if, after 180 days from such termination, Artist has not retaken possession of the artworks covered by this Agreement, title to said works and/or to the proceeds therefrom shall vest in Gallery.

6. Sole and Entire Agreement

This written Agreement contains the sole and entire Consignment Agreement between the parties and shall supersede any and all other agreements between the parties. The parties acknowledge and agree that neither of them has made any representations, including the execution and delivery hereof, except such representations as are specifically set forth herein and each of the parties hereto acknowledge that he or it has relied on his or its own judgment in entering into the same. The parties hereto further acknowledge that any statements or representations that may have heretofore been made by either of them to the other are void and of no effect and that neither of them has relied thereon in connection with his or its dealings with the other.

7. No Waiver or Modification

It is further agreed that no waiver or modification of this Agreement or of any covenant, condition or limitation herein contained shall be valid unless in writing and duly executed by the party to be charged therewith and that no evidence of any waiver or modification shall be offered or received in evidence in any proceeding, arbitration or litigation between the parties hereto arising out of or affecting this Agreement, or the rights or obligations of any party hereunder, unless such waiver or modification is in writing, duly executed as aforesaid, and the parties further agree that the provisions of this paragraph 7 may not be waived, except as herein set forth.

8. Notices

Any notice required or permitted to be given under this Agreement shall be sufficient, if in writing, and if sent by certified mail, return receipt requested, to the following addresses:

Artist:

Gallery:

9.

IN WITNESS WHEREOF, the parties hereto have executed this Agreement on the date and year first above written.

Address   ARTIST: _____

                            GALLERY: _____

                                By _____

Address

---

*Based on a document developed by the Council for Assistance to the Arts [Los Angeles].

E AGREEMENT BETWEEN ARTIST AND RENTAL SALES GALLERY—
PORTLAND ART MUSEUM

Date _____

The Artist agrees that upon the selection of a work of art by the Art Selection Committee of the Rental–Sales Gallery of the Portland Art Museum, such work may be rented by the Rental–Sales Gallery to any member of the Portland Art Association and may be sold pursuant to the terms of the agreement of the Rental–Sales Gallery. The Artist shall keep the Rental–Sales Gallery informed of all changes in his address or that of his agent.

The full agreement of the Rental–Sales Gallery is made a part of this contract by reference and is available to all artists upon request. Pertinent parts appear on the reverse of this contract.

Signature _____

Agent _____   Name _____

Address _____   Address _____

City _____ Zip _____   City _____ Zip ____

Phone _____   Phone _____

Signed _____
        (Rental–Sales Gallery Representative

The artist agrees to the Rental or Sale of the works of art and their values listed below:

R–S Catalog
  Number   Title   Size   Medium   Value
(RSG No. will be
 Listed by RSG.)

_____ _____

_____ _____

_____ _____

_____ _____

(over)

The Art Selection Committee of the Rental Sales Gallery of the
Portland Art Association shall determine which artists shall be invited to submit works for the
Rental Sales inventory and which works shall be accepted. The Gallery specifically reserves
the option to request withdrawal of any artist if he does not submit work, upon invitation, for
a period of two years.

If a work is not rented within six months, or it is otherwise determined by the Gallery
that a work should be withdrawn, the artist, upon being notified, shall withdraw such work
within ten days unless other arrangements are made.

Delivery and pickup of works to and from the Gallery shall be the responsibility of the
artist.

The artist may at any time withdraw from the Rental Sales Gallery a work that is not
rented. The artist may not withdraw a work which is rented until the expiration of the rental
period, the renter having the option to purchase during the term of his rental.

Artist's fees for rentals shall be based on the value of the work of art and shall follow
a posted fee schedule. The Rental Sales Gallery shall pay all artist's rental fees to artists
monthly. If the renter decides to purchase during the rental period (not to exceed six
months), the artist's fees previously paid shall apply to the purchase price.

The Rental Sales Gallery shall receive a percentage of the sale price of all works sold
while in the inventory of the Gallery. The artist agrees that payment for such sales may be
made on an installment basis, terms to be arranged by the Gallery. Rental Sales commission
shall be deducted from the cash payment of the first installment and all subsequent
installment payments until said commission is paid in full. The Rental Sales Gallery shall
forward non-commissionable payments from purchasers to the artists monthly.

The terms of this agreement, or any purchase contract rising from this agreement, shall
be binding on the heirs or personal representatives of the artist.

Art works are fully insured by the Portland Art Association from the time of delivery
to the Rental Sales Gallery until returned to the artist or until purchased for cash or on
contract.

The Rental Sales Gallery shall have the option and responsibility for arrangement of
art work for openings and daily display.

APPENDIX F
FORM VA

Detach and read these instructions before completing this form. Make sure all applicable spaces have been filled in before you return this form.

BASIC INFORMATION

When to Use This Form: Use Form VA for copyright registration of published or unpublished works of the visual arts. This category consists of "pictorial, graphic, or sculptural works," including two-dimensional and three-dimensional works of fine, graphic, and applied art, photographs, prints and art reproductions, maps, globes, charts, technical drawings, diagrams, and models.

What Does Copyright Protect? Copyright in a work of the visual arts protects those pictorial, graphic, or sculptural elements that, either alone or in combination, represent an "original work of authorship." The statute declares: "In no case does copyright protection for an original work of authorship extend to any idea, procedure, process, system, method of operation, concept, principle, or discovery, regardless of the form in which it is described, explained, illustrated, or embodied in such work."

Works of Artistic Craftsmanship and Designs: "Works of artistic craftsmanship" are registrable on Form VA, but the statute makes clear that protection extends to "their form" and not to "their mechanical or utilitarian aspects." The "design of a useful article" is considered copyrightable "only if, and only to the extent that, such design incorporates pictorial, graphic, or sculptural features that can be identified separately from, and are capable of existing independently of, the utilitarian aspects of the article."

Labels and Advertisements: Works prepared for use in connection with the sale or advertisement of goods and services are registrable if they contain "original work of authorship." Use Form VA if the copyrightable mate. al in the work you are registering is mainly pictorial or graphic; use Form TX if it consists mainly of text. **NOTE:** Words and short phrases such as names, titles, and slogans cannot be protected by copyright, and the same is true of standard symbols, emblems, and other commonly used graphic designs that are in the public domain. When used commercially, material of that sort can sometimes be protected under state laws of unfair competition or under the Federal trademark laws. For information about trademark registration, write to the Commissioner of Patents and Trademarks, Washington, D.C. 20231.

Deposit to Accompany Application: An application for copyright registration must be accompanied by a deposit consisting of copies representing the entire work for which registration is to be made.

Unpublished Work: Deposit one complete copy.

Published Work: Deposit two complete copies of the best edition.

Work First Published Outside the United States: Deposit one complete copy of the first foreign edition.

Contribution to a Collective Work: Deposit one complete copy of the best edition of the collective work.

The Copyright Notice: For published works, the law provides that a copyright notice in a specified form "shall be placed on all publicly distributed copies from which the work can be visually perceived." Use of the copyright notice is the responsibility of the copyright owner and does not require advance permission from the Copyright Office. The required form of the notice for copies generally consists of three elements: (1) the symbol "©", or the word "Copyright," or the abbreviation "Copr."; (2) the year of first publication; and (3) the name of the owner of copyright. For example: "© 1981 Constance Porter." The notice is to be affixed to the copies "in such manner and location as to give reasonable notice of the claim of copyright."

For further information about copyright registration, notice, or special questions relating to copyright problems, write:
Information and Publications Section, LM-455
Copyright Office, Library of Congress, Washington, D.C. 20559

PRIVACY ACT ADVISORY STATEMENT Required by the Privacy Act of 1974 (P.L. 93-579)
The authority for requesting this information is title 17, U.S.C., secs. 409 and 410. Furnishing the requested information is voluntary. But if the information is not furnished, it may be necessary to delay or refuse registration and you may not be entitled to certain relief, remedies, and benefits provided in chapters 4 and 5 of title 17, U.S.C.
The principal uses of the requested information are the establishment and maintenance of a public record and the examination of the application for compliance with legal requirements
Other routine uses include public inspection and copying, preparation of public indexes, preparation of public catalogs of copyright registrations, and preparation of search reports upon request
NOTE: No other advisory statement will be given in connection with this application. Please keep this statement and refer to it if we communicate with you regarding this application

LINE-BY-LINE INSTRUCTIONS

1 SPACE 1: Title

Title of This Work: Every work submitted for copyright registration must be given a title to identify that particular work. If the copies of the work bear a title (or an identifying phrase that could serve as a title), transcribe that wording *completely* and *exactly* on the application. Indexing of the registration and future identification of the work will depend on the information you give here.

Previous or Alternative Titles: Complete this space if there are any additional titles for the work under which someone searching for the registration might be likely to look, or under which a document pertaining to the work might be recorded.

Publication as a Contribution: If the work being registered is a contribution to a periodical, serial, or collection, give the title of the contribution in the "Title of This Work" space. Then, in the line headed "Publication as a Contribution," give information about the collective work in which the contribution appeared.

Nature of This Work: Briefly describe the general nature or character of the pictorial, graphic, or sculptural work being registered for copyright. Examples: "Oil Painting"; "Charcoal Drawing"; "Etching"; "Sculpture"; "Map"; "Photograph"; "Scale Model"; "Lithographic Print"; "Jewelry Design"; "Fabric Design."

2 SPACE 2: Author(s)

General Instructions: After reading these instructions, decide who are the "authors" of this work for copyright purposes. Then, unless the work is a "collective work," give the requested information about every "author" who contributed any appreciable amount of copyrightable matter to this version of the work. If you need further space, request additional Continuation Sheets. In the case of a collective work, such as a catalog of paintings or collection of cartoons by various authors, give information about the author of the collective work as a whole.

Name of Author: The fullest form of the author's name should be given. Unless the work was "made for hire," the individual who actually created the work is its "author." In the case of a work made for hire, the statute provides that "the employer or other person for whom the work was prepared is considered the author."

What is a "Work Made for Hire"? A "work made for hire" is defined as: (1) "a work prepared by an employee within the scope of his or her employment"; or (2) "a work specially ordered or commissioned for use as a contribution to a collective work, as a part of a motion picture or other audiovisual work, as a translation, as a supplementary work, as a compilation, as an instructional text, as a test, as answer material for a test, or as an atlas, if the parties expressly agree in a written instrument signed by them that the work shall be considered a work made for hire." If you have checked "Yes" to indicate that the work was "made for hire," you must give the full legal name of the employer (or other person for whom the work was prepared). You may also include the name of the employee along with the name of the employer (for example: "Elster Publishing Co., employer for hire of John Ferguson").

"Anonymous" or "Pseudonymous" Work: An author's contribution to a work is "anonymous" if that author is not identified on the copies or phonorecords of the work. An author's contribution to a work is "pseudonymous" if that author is identified on the copies or phonorecords under a fictitious name. If the work is "anonymous" you may: (1) leave the line blank; or (2) state "anonymous" on the line; or (3) reveal the author's identity. If the work is "pseudonymous" you may: (1) leave the line blank; or (2) give the pseudonym and identify it as such (for example: "Huntley Haverstock, pseudonym"); or (3) reveal the author's name, making clear which is the real name and which is the pseudonym (for example: "Henry Leek, whose pseudonym is Priam Farrel"). However, the citizenship or domicile of the author **must** be given in all cases.

Dates of Birth and Death: If the author is dead, the statute requires that the year of death be included in the application unless the work is anonymous or pseudonymous. The author's birth date is optional, but is useful as a form of identification. Leave this space blank if the author's contribution was a "work made for hire."

130

Author's Nationality or Domicile: Give the country of which the author is a citizen, or the country in which the author is domiciled. Nationality or domicile **must** be given in all cases.

Nature of Authorship: Give a brief general statement of the nature of this particular author's contribution to the work. Examples: "Painting"; "Photograph"; "Silk Screen Reproduction"; "Co-author of Cartographic Material"; "Technical Drawing"; "Text and Artwork."

3 SPACE 3: Creation and Publication

General Instructions: Do not confuse "creation" with "publication." Every application for copyright registration must state "the year in which creation of the work was completed." Give the date and nation of first publication only if the work has been published.

Creation: Under the statute, a work is "created" when it is fixed in a copy or phonorecord for the first time. Where a work has been prepared over a period of time, the part of the work existing in fixed form on a particular date constitutes the created work on that date. The date you give here should be the year in which the author completed the particular version for which registration is now being sought, even if other versions exist or if further changes or additions are planned.

Publication: The statute defines "publication" as "the distribution of copies or phonorecords of a work to the public by sale or other transfer of ownership, or by rental, lease, or lending"; a work is also "published" if there has been an "offering to distribute copies or phonorecords to a group of persons for purposes of further distribution, public performance, or public display." Give the full date (month, day, year) when, and the country where, publication first occurred. If first publication took place simultaneously in the United States and other countries, it is sufficient to state "U.S.A."

4 SPACE 4: Claimant(s)

Name(s) and Address(es) of Copyright Claimant(s): Give the name(s) and address(es) of the copyright claimant(s) in this work even if the claimant is the same as the author. Copyright in a work belongs initially to the author of the work (including, in the case of a work made for hire, the employer or other person for whom the work was prepared). The copyright claimant is either the author of the work or a person or organization to whom the copyright initially belonging to the author has been transferred.

Transfer: The statute provides that, if the copyright claimant is not the author, the application for registration must contain "a brief statement of how the claimant obtained ownership of the copyright." If any copyright claimant named in space 4 is not an author named in space 2, give a brief, general statement summarizing the means by which that claimant obtained ownership of the copyright. Examples: "By written contract"; "Transfer of all rights by author"; "Assignment"; "By will." Do not attach transfer documents or other attachments or riders.

5 SPACE 5: Previous Registration

General Instructions: The questions in space 5 are intended to find out whether an earlier registration has been made for this work and, if so, whether there is any basis for a new registration. As a rule, only one basic copyright registration can be made for the same version of a particular work.

Same Version: If this version is substantially the same as the work covered by a previous registration, a second registration is not generally possible unless: (1) the work has been registered in unpublished form and a second registration is now being sought to cover this first published edition; or (2) some-

one other than the author is identified as copyright claimant in the earlier registration, and the author is now seeking registration in his or her own name. If either of these two exceptions apply, check the appropriate box and give the earlier registration number and date. Otherwise, do not submit Form VA; instead, write the Copyright Office for information about supplementary registration or recordation of transfers of copyright ownership.

Changed Version: If the work has been changed, and you are now seeking registration to cover the additions or revisions, check the last box in space 5, give the earlier registration number and date, and complete both parts of space 6 in accordance with the instructions below.

Previous Registration Number and Date: If more than one previous registration has been made for the work, give the number and date of the latest registration.

6 SPACE 6: Derivative Work or Compilation

General Instructions: Complete space 6 if this work is a "changed version," "compilation," or "derivative work," and if it incorporates one or more earlier works that have already been published or registered for copyright, or that have fallen into the public domain. A "compilation" is defined as "a work formed by the collection and assembling of preexisting materials or of data that are selected, coordinated, or arranged in such a way that the resulting work as a whole constitutes an original work of authorship." A "derivative work" is "a work based on one or more preexisting works." Examples of derivative works include reproductions of works of art, sculptures based on drawings, lithographs based on paintings, maps based on previously published sources, or "any other form in which a work may be recast, transformed, or adapted." Derivative works also include works "consisting of editorial revisions, annotations, or other modifications" if these changes, as a whole, represent an original work of authorship.

Preexisting Material (space 6a): Complete this space **and** space 6b for derivative works. In this space identify the preexisting work that has been recast, transformed, or adapted. Examples of preexisting material might be "Grunewald Altarpiece"; or "19th century quilt design." Do not complete this space for compilations.

Material Added to This Work (space 6b): Give a brief, general statement of the **additional** new material covered by the copyright claim for which registration is sought. In the case of a derivative work, identify this new material. Examples: "Adaptation of design and additional artistic work"; "Reproduction of painting by photolithography"; "Additional cartographic material"; "Compilation of photographs." If the work is a compilation, give a brief, general statement describing both the material that has been compiled **and** the compilation itself. Example: "Compilation of 19th Century Political Cartoons."

7,8,9 SPACE 7, 8, 9: Fee, Correspondence, Certification, Return Address

Deposit Account: If you maintain a Deposit Account in the Copyright Office, identify it in space 7. Otherwise leave the space blank and send the fee of $10 with your application and deposit.

Correspondence (space 7): This space should contain the name, address, area code, and telephone number of the person to be consulted if correspondence about this application becomes necessary.

Certification (space 8): The application cannot be accepted unless it bears the date and the **handwritten signature** of the author or other copyright claimant, or of the owner of exclusive right(s), or of the duly authorized agent of the author, claimant, or owner of exclusive right(s).

Address for Return of Certificate (space 9): The address box must be completed legibly since the certificate will be returned in a window envelope.

MORE INFORMATION

Form of Deposit for Works of the Visual Arts

Exceptions to General Deposit Requirements: As explained on the reverse side of this page, the statutory deposit requirements (generally one copy for unpublished works and two copies for published works) will vary for particular kinds of works of the visual arts. The copyright law authorizes the Register of Copyrights to issue regulations specifying "the administrative classes into which works are to be placed for purposes of deposit and registration, and the nature of the copies or phonorecords to be deposited in the various classes specified." For particular classes, the regulations may require or permit "the deposit of identifying material instead of copies or phonorecords," or "the deposit of only one copy or phonorecord where two would normally be required."

What Should You Deposit? The detailed requirements with respect to the kind of deposit to accompany an application on Form VA are contained in the Copyright

Office Regulations. The following does not cover all of the deposit requirements, but is intended to give you some general guidance.

For an Unpublished Work, the material deposited should represent the entire copyrightable content of the work for which registration is being sought.

For a Published Work, the material deposited should generally consist of two complete copies of the best edition. Exceptions: (1) For certain types of works, one complete copy may be deposited instead of two. These include greeting cards, postcards, stationery, labels, advertisements, scientific drawings, and globes; (2) For most three-dimensional sculptural works, and for certain two-dimensional works, the Copyright Office Regulations require deposit of identifying material (photographs or drawings in a specified form) rather than copies; and (3) Under certain circumstances, for works published in five copies or less or in limited, numbered editions, the deposit may consist of one copy or of identifying reproductions.

FORM VA
UNITED STATES COPYRIGHT OFFICE

REGISTRATION NUMBER

_____

VA   VAU

_____
EFFECTIVE DATE OF REGISTRATION

_____

Month   Day   Year

DO NOT WRITE ABOVE THIS LINE. IF YOU NEED MORE SPACE, USE A SEPARATE CONTINUATION SHEET.

1   **TITLE OF THIS WORK ▼**   **NATURE OF THIS WORK ▼** See instructions

PREVIOUS OR ALTERNATIVE TITLES ▼

PUBLICATION AS A CONTRIBUTION   If this work was published as a contribution to a periodical, serial, or collection, give information about the collective work in which the contribution appeared.   **Title of Collective Work ▼**

If published in a periodical or serial give: **Volume ▼**   **Number ▼**   **Issue Date ▼**   **On Pages ▼**

2   **a**

NAME OF AUTHOR ▼   **DATES OF BIRTH AND DEATH**
Year Born ▼   Year Died ▼

Was this contribution to the work a "work made for hire"?
☐ Yes
☐ No

AUTHOR'S NATIONALITY OR DOMICILE
Name of Country
OR { Citizen of ▶_____
     Domiciled in ▶_____

WAS THIS AUTHOR'S CONTRIBUTION TO THE WORK
Anonymous? ☐ Yes ☐ No
Pseudonymous? ☐ Yes ☐ No

If the answer to either of these questions is "Yes," see detailed instructions.

NATURE OF AUTHORSHIP   Briefly describe nature of the material created by this author in which copyright is claimed. ▼

NOTE

Under the law, the "author" of a "work made for hire" is generally the employer, not the employee (see instructions). For any part of this work that was "made for hire" check "Yes" in the space provided, give the employer (or other person for whom the work was prepared) as "Author" of that part, and leave the space for dates of birth and death blank.

b

NAME OF AUTHOR ▼   **DATES OF BIRTH AND DEATH**
Year Born ▼   Year Died ▼

Was this contribution to the work a "work made for hire"?
☐ Yes
☐ No

AUTHOR'S NATIONALITY OR DOMICILE
Name of country
OR { Citizen of ▶_____
     Domiciled in ▶_____

WAS THIS AUTHOR'S CONTRIBUTION TO THE WORK
Anonymous? ☐ Yes ☐ No
Pseudonymous? ☐ Yes ☐ No

If the answer to either of these questions is "Yes," see detailed instructions.

NATURE OF AUTHORSHIP   Briefly describe nature of the material created by this author in which copyright is claimed. ▼

c

NAME OF AUTHOR ▼   **DATES OF BIRTH AND DEATH**
Year Born ▼   Year Died ▼

Was this contribution to the work a "work made for hire"?
☐ Yes
☐ No

AUTHOR'S NATIONALITY OR DOMICILE
Name of Country
OR { Citizen of ▶_____
     Domiciled in ▶_____

WAS THIS AUTHOR'S CONTRIBUTION TO THE WORK
Anonymous? ☐ Yes ☐ No
Pseudonymous? ☐ Yes ☐ No

If the answer to either of these questions is "Yes," see detailed instructions.

NATURE OF AUTHORSHIP   Briefly describe nature of the material created by this author in which copyright is claimed. ▼

3   **YEAR IN WHICH CREATION OF THIS WORK WAS COMPLETED** This information must be given in all cases.   ◀ Year

DATE AND NATION OF FIRST PUBLICATION OF THIS PARTICULAR WORK
Complete this information ONLY if this work has been published.   Month ▶_____ Day ▶_____ Year ▶_____ ◀ Nation

4

See instructions before completing this space.

COPYRIGHT CLAIMANT(S) Name and address must be given even if the claimant is the same as the author given in space 2.▼

TRANSFER If the claimant(s) named here in space 4 are different from the author(s) named in space 2, give a brief statement of how the claimant(s) obtained ownership of the copyright.▼

DO NOT WRITE HERE OFFICE USE ONLY

APPLICATION RECEIVED

ONE DEPOSIT RECEIVED

TWO DEPOSITS RECEIVED

REMITTANCE NUMBER AND DATE

MORE ON BACK ▶
• Complete all applicable spaces (numbers 5-9) on the reverse side of this page.
• See detailed instructions.   • Sign the form at line 8.

DO NOT WRITE HERE

Page 1 of_____pages

DO NOT WRITE ABOVE THIS LINE. IF YOU NEED MORE SPACE, USE A SEPARATE CONTINUATION SHEET.

PREVIOUS REGISTRATION Has registration for this work, or for an earlier version of this work, already been made in the Copyright Office?

☐ **Yes** ☐ **No** If your answer is "Yes," why is another registration being sought? (Check appropriate box) ▼

☐ This is the first published edition of a work previously registered in unpublished form.

☐ This is the first application submitted by this author as copyright claimant.

☐ This is a changed version of the work, as shown by space 6 on this application.

If your answer is "Yes," give: **Previous Registration Number** ▼   **Year of Registration** ▼

5

DERIVATIVE WORK OR COMPILATION Complete both space 6a & 6b for a derivative work; complete only 6b for a compilation.

a. Preexisting Material Identify any preexisting work or works that this work is based on or incorporates. ▼

_____

_____

b. Material Added to This Work Give a brief, general statement of the material that has been added to this work and in which copyright is claimed.▼

_____

_____

6

See instructions
before completing
this space.

DEPOSIT ACCOUNT If the registration fee is to be charged to a Deposit Account established in the Copyright Office, give name and number of Account.

Name ▼   **Account Number** ▼

_____   _____

7

CORRESPONDENCE Give name and address to which correspondence about this application should be sent.   Name/Address/Apt/City/State/Zip ▼

_____

_____

_____

                    Area Code & Telephone Number ▶

Be sure to
give your
daytime phone
◀ number.

8

CERTIFICATION* I, the undersigned, hereby certify that I am the

Check only one ▼

☐ author

☐ other copyright claimant

☐ owner of exclusive right(s)

☐ authorized agent of_____
                    Name of author or other copyright claimant, or owner of exclusive right(s) ▲

of the work identified in this application and that the statements made
by me in this application are correct to the best of my knowledge.

Typed or printed name and date ▼ If this is a published work, this date must be the same as or later than the date of publication given in space 3.

_____   _date ▶ _____

☞ Handwritten signature (X) ▼

9

**MAIL
CERTIFI-
CATE TO**

Name ▼

Number/Street/Apartment Number ▼

City/State/ZIP ▼

**Certificate
will be
mailed in
window
envelope**

Have you:
● Completed all necessary
  spaces?
● Signed your application in space
  8?
● Enclosed check or money order
  for $10 payable to *Register of
  Copyrights*?
● Enclosed your deposit material
  with the application and fee?

MAIL TO: Register of Copyrights,
Library of Congress, Washington,
D.C. 20559.

133

Detach and read these instructions before completing this form. Make sure all applicable spaces have been filled in before you return this form.

BASIC INFORMATION

When to Use This Form: Use Form TX for registration of published or unpublished non-dramatic literary works, excluding periodicals or serial issues. This class includes a wide variety of works: fiction, non-fiction, poetry, textbooks, reference works, directories, catalogs, advertising copy, compilations of information, and computer programs. For periodicals and serials, use Form SE.

Deposit to Accompany Application: An application for copyright registration must be accompanied by a deposit consisting of copies or phonorecords representing the entire work for which registration is to be made. The following are the general deposit requirements as set forth in the statute:

Unpublished Work: Deposit one complete copy (or phonorecord).

Published Work: Deposit two complete copies (or phonorecords) of the best edition.

Work First Published Outside the United States: Deposit one complete copy (or phonorecord) of the first foreign edition.

Contribution to a Collective Work: Deposit one complete copy (or phonorecord) of the best edition of the collective work.

The Copyright Notice: For published works, the law provides that a copyright notice in a specified form "shall be placed on all publicly distributed copies from which the work can be visually perceived." Use of the copyright notice is the responsibility of the copyright owner and does not require advance permission from the Copyright Office. The required form of the notice for copies generally consists of three elements: (1) the symbol "©", or the word "Copyright," or the abbreviation "Copr."; (2) the year of first publication; and (3) the name of the owner of copyright. For example: "© 1981 Constance Porter." The notice is to be affixed to the copies "in such manner and location as to give reasonable notice of the claim of copyright."

For further information about copyright registration, notice, or special questions relating to copyright problems, write:

Information and Publications Section, LM-455
Copyright Office
Library of Congress
Washington, D.C. 20559

PRIVACY ACT ADVISORY STATEMENT **Required by the Privacy Act of 1974 (Public Law 93-579)**	PRINCIPAL USES OF REQUESTED INFORMATION • Establishment and maintenance of a public record • Examination of the application for compliance with legal requirements
AUTHORITY FOR REQUESTING THIS INFORMATION • Title 17, U.S.C., Secs. 409 and 410	OTHER ROUTINE USES • Public inspection and copying • Preparation of public indexes
FURNISHING THE REQUESTED INFORMATION IS • Voluntary	• Preparation of public catalogs of copyright registrations • Preparation of search reports upon request
BUT IF THE INFORMATION IS NOT FURNISHED • It may be necessary to delay or refuse registration • You may not be entitled to certain relief, remedies, and benefits provided in chapters 4 and 5 of title 17, U.S.C.	NOTE • No other advisory statement will be given you in connection with this application • Please keep this statement and refer to it if we communicate with you regarding this application

LINE-BY-LINE INSTRUCTIONS

1 SPACE 1: Title

Title of This Work: Every work submitted for copyright registration must be given a title to identify that particular work. If the copies or phonorecords of the work bear a title (or an identifying phrase that could serve as a title), transcribe that wording *completely* and *exactly* on the application. Indexing of the registration and future identification of the work will depend on the information you give here.

Previous or Alternative Titles: Complete this space if there are any additional titles for the work under which someone searching for the registration might be likely to look, or under which a document pertaining to the work might be recorded.

Publication as a Contribution: If the work being registered is a contribution to a periodical, serial, or collection, give the title of the contribution in the "Title of this Work" space. Then, in the line headed "Publication as a Contribution," give information about the collective work in which the contribution appeared.

2 SPACE 2: Author(s)

General Instructions: After reading these instructions, decide who are the "authors" of this work for copyright purposes. Then, unless the work is a "collective work," give the requested information about every "author" who contributed any appreciable amount of copyrightable matter to this version of the work. If you need further space, request additional Continuation sheets. In the case of a collective work, such as an anthology, collection of essays, or encyclopedia, give information about the author of the collective work as a whole.

Name of Author: The fullest form of the author's name should be given. Unless the work was "made for hire," the individual who actually created the work is its "author." In the case of a work made for hire, the statute provides that "the employer or other person for whom the work was prepared is considered the author."

What is a "Work Made for Hire"? A "work made for hire" is defined as: (1) "a work prepared by an employee within the scope of his or her employment"; or (2) "a work specially ordered or commissioned for use as a contribution to a collective work, as a part of a motion picture or other audiovisual work, as a translation, as a supplementary work, as a compilation, as an instructional text, as a test, as answer material for a test, or as an atlas, if the parties expressly agree in a written instrument signed by them that the work shall be considered a work made for hire." If you have checked "Yes" to indicate that the work was "made for hire," you must give the full legal name of the employer (or other person for whom the work was prepared). You may also include the name of the employee along with the name of the employer (for example: "Elster Publishing Co., employer for hire of John Ferguson").

"Anonymous" or "Pseudonymous" Work: An author's contribution to a work is "anonymous" if that author is not identified on the copies or phonorecords of the work. An author's contribution to a work is "pseudonymous" if that author is identified on the copies or phonorecords under a fictitious name. If the work is "anonymous" you may: (1) leave the line blank; or (2) state " anonymous" on the line; or (3) reveal the author's identity. If the work is "pseudonymous" you may : (1) leave the line blank; or (2) give the pseudonym and identify it as such (for example: "Huntley Haverstock, pseudonym"); or (3) reveal the author's name, making clear which is the real name and which is the pseudonym (for example: "Judith Barton, whose pseudonym is Madeline Elster"). However, the citizenship or domicile of the author **must** be given in all cases.

Dates of Birth and Death: If the author is dead, the statute requires that the year of death be included in the application unless the work is anonymous or pseudonymous. The author's birth date is optional, but is useful as a form of identification. Leave this space blank if the author's contribution was a "work made for hire."

Author's Nationality or Domicile: Give the country of which the author is a citizen, or the country in which the author is domiciled. Nationality or domicile **must** be given in all cases.

Nature of Authorship: After the words "Nature of Authorship" give a brief general statement of the nature of this particular author's contribution to the work. Examples: "Entire text"; "Coauthor of entire text"; "Chapters 11-14"; "Editorial revisions"; "Compilation and English translation"; "New text."

3 SPACE 3: Creation and Publication

General Instructions: Do not confuse "creation" with "publication." Every application for copyright registration must state "the year in which creation of the work was completed." Give the date and nation of first publication only if the work has been published.

Creation: Under the statute, a work is "created" when it is fixed in a copy or phonorecord for the first time. Where a work has been prepared over a period of time, the part of the work existing in fixed form on a particular date constitutes the created work on that date. The date you give here should be the year in which the author completed the particular version for which registration is now being sought, even if other versions exist or if further changes or additions are planned.

Publication: The statute defines "publication" as "the distribution of copies or phonorecords of a work to the public by sale or other transfer of ownership, or by rental, lease, or lending"; a work is also "published" if there has been an "offering to distribute copies or phonorecords to a group of persons for purposes of further distribution, public performance, or public display." Give the full date (month, day, year) when, and the country where, publication first occurred. If first publication took place simultaneously in the United States and other countries, it is sufficient to state "U.S.A."

4 SPACE 4: Claimant(s)

Name(s) and Address(es) of Copyright Claimant(s): Give the name(s) and address(es) of the copyright claimant(s) in this work even if the claimant is the same as the author. Copyright in a work belongs initially to the author of the work (including, in the case of a work made for hire, the employer or other person for whom the work was prepared). The copyright claimant is either the author of the work or a person or organization to whom the copyright initially belonging to the author has been transferred.

Transfer: The statute provides that, if the copyright claimant is not the author, the application for registration must contain "a brief statement of how the claimant obtained ownership of the copyright." If any copyright claimant named in space 4 is not an author named in space 2, give a brief, general statement summarizing the means by which that claimant obtained ownership of the copyright. Examples: "By written contract"; "Transfer of all rights by author"; "Assignment"; "By will." Do not attach transfer documents or other attachments or riders.

5 SPACE 5: Previous Registration

General Instructions: The questions in space 5 are intended to find out whether an earlier registration has been made for this work and, if so, whether there is any basis for a new registration. As a general rule, only one basic copyright registration can be made for the same version of a particular work.

Same Version: If this version is substantially the same as the work covered by a previous registration, a second registration is not generally possible unless: (1) the work has been registered in unpublished form and a second registration is now being sought to cover this first published edition; or (2) someone other than the author is identified as copyright claimant in the earlier registration, and the author is now seeking registration in his or her own name. If either of these two exceptions apply, check the appropriate box and give the earlier registration number and date. Otherwise, do not submit Form TX; instead, write the Copyright Office for information about supplementary registration or recordation of transfers of copyright ownership.

Changed Version: If the work has been changed, and you are now seeking registration to cover the additions or revisions, check the last box in space 5, give the earlier registration number and date, and complete both parts of space 6 in accordance with the instructions below.

Previous Registration Number and Date: If more than one previous registration has been made for the work, give the number and date of the latest registration.

6 SPACE 6: Derivative Work or Compilation

General Instructions: Complete space 6 if this work is a "changed version," "compilation," or "derivative work," and if it incorporates one or more earlier works that have already been published or registered for copyright, or that have fallen into the public domain. A "compilation" is defined as "a work formed by the collection and assembling of preexisting materials or of data that are selected, coordinated, or arranged in such a way that the resulting work as

a whole constitutes an original work of authorship." A "derivative work" is "a work based on one or more preexisting works." Examples of derivative works include translations, fictionalizations, abridgments, condensations, or "any other form in which a work may be recast, transformed, or adapted." Derivative works also include works "consisting of editorial revisions, annotations, or other modifications" if these changes, as a whole, represent an original work of authorship.

Preexisting Material (space 6a): For derivative works, complete this space **and** space 6b. In space 6a identify the preexisting work that has been recast, transformed, or adapted. An example of preexisting material might be: "Russian version of Goncharov's 'Oblomov'." Do not complete space 6a for compilations.

Material Added to This Work (space 6b): Give a brief, general statement of the new material covered by the copyright claim for which registration is sought. **Derivative work** examples include: "Foreword, editing, critical annotations"; "Translation"; "Chapters 11-17." If the work is a **compilation**, describe both the compilation itself and the material that has been compiled. Example: "Compilation of certain 1917 Speeches by Woodrow Wilson." A work may be both a derivative work and compilation, in which case a sample statement might be: "Compilation and additional new material."

7 SPACE 7: Manufacturing Provisions

Due to the expiration of the Manufacturing Clause of the copyright law on June 30, 1986, this space has been deleted.

8 SPACE 8: Reproduction for Use of Blind or Physically Handicapped Individuals

General Instructions: One of the major programs of the Library of Congress is to provide Braille editions and special recordings of works for the exclusive use of the blind and physically handicapped. In an effort to simplify and speed up the copyright licensing procedures that are a necessary part of this program, section 710 of the copyright statute provides for the establishment of a voluntary licensing system to be tied in with copyright registration. Copyright Office regulations provide that you may grant a license for such reproduction and distribution solely for the use of persons who are certified by competent authority as unable to read normal printed material as a result of physical limitations. The license is entirely voluntary, nonexclusive, and may be terminated upon 90 days notice.

How to Grant the License: If you wish to grant it, check one of the three boxes in space 8. Your check in one of these boxes, together with your signature in space 10, will mean that the Library of Congress can proceed to reproduce and distribute under the license without further paperwork. For further information, write for Circular R63.

9,10,11 SPACE 9, 10, 11: Fee, Correspondence, Certification, Return Address

Deposit Account: If you maintain a Deposit Account in the Copyright Office, identify it in space 9. Otherwise leave the space blank and send the fee of $10 with your application and deposit.

Correspondence (space 9): This space should contain the name, address, area code, and telephone number of the person to be consulted if correspondence about this application becomes necessary.

Certification (space 10): The application can not be accepted unless it bears the date and the **handwritten signature** of the author or other copyright claimant, or of the owner of exclusive right(s), or of the duly authorized agent of author, claimant, or owner of exclusive right(s).

Address for Return of Certificate (space 11): The address box must be completed legibly since the certificate will be returned in a window envelope.

FORM TX

UNITED STATES COPYRIGHT OFFICE

REGISTRATION NUMBER
_____

TX   TXU
_____
EFFECTIVE DATE OF REGISTRATION

_____
Month   Day   Year

DO NOT WRITE ABOVE THIS LINE. IF YOU NEED MORE SPACE, USE A SEPARATE CONTINUATION SHEET.

1

TITLE OF THIS WORK ▼

PREVIOUS OR ALTERNATIVE TITLES ▼

PUBLICATION AS A CONTRIBUTION If this work was published as a contribution to a periodical, serial, or collection, give information about the collective work in which the contribution appeared.   **Title of Collective Work ▼**

If published in a periodical or serial give: **Volume ▼**   **Number ▼**   **Issue Date ▼**   **On Pages ▼**

2

a

NAME OF AUTHOR ▼

DATES OF BIRTH AND DEATH
Year Born ▼   Year Died ▼

Was this contribution to the work a "work made for hire"?
☐ Yes
☐ No

AUTHOR'S NATIONALITY OR DOMICILE
Name of Country
OR { Citizen of ▶_____
     Domiciled in ▶_____

WAS THIS AUTHOR'S CONTRIBUTION TO THE WORK
Anonymous?   ☐ Yes ☐ No
Pseudonymous?   ☐ Yes ☐ No
If the answer to either of these questions is "Yes," see detailed instructions.

NATURE OF AUTHORSHIP Briefly describe nature of the material created by this author in which copyright is claimed. ▼

NOTE

Under the law. the "author" of a "work made for hire" is generally the employer. not the employee (see instructions) For any part of this work that was "made for hire" check "Yes" in the space provided. give the employer (or other person for whom the work was prepared) as "Author" of that part. and leave the space for dates of birth and death blank.

b

NAME OF AUTHOR ▼

DATES OF BIRTH AND DEATH
Year Born ▼   Year Died ▼

Was this contribution to the work a "work made for hire"?
☐ Yes
☐ No

AUTHOR'S NATIONALITY OR DOMICILE
Name of country
OR { Citizen of ▶_____
     Domiciled in ▶_____

WAS THIS AUTHOR'S CONTRIBUTION TO THE WORK
Anonymous?   ☐ Yes ☐ No
Pseudonymous?   ☐ Yes ☐ No
If the answer to either of these questions is "Yes," see detailed instructions.

NATURE OF AUTHORSHIP Briefly describe nature of the material created by this author in which copyright is claimed. ▼

c

NAME OF AUTHOR ▼

DATES OF BIRTH AND DEATH
Year Born ▼   Year Died ▼

Was this contribution to the work a "work made for hire"?
☐ Yes
☐ No

AUTHOR'S NATIONALITY OR DOMICILE
Name of Country
OR { Citizen of ▶_____
     Domiciled in ▶_____

WAS THIS AUTHOR'S CONTRIBUTION TO THE WORK
Anonymous?   ☐ Yes ☐ No
Pseudonymous?   ☐ Yes ☐ No
If the answer to either of these questions is "Yes," see detailed instructions.

NATURE OF AUTHORSHIP Briefly describe nature of the material created by this author in which copyright is claimed. ▼

3

YEAR IN WHICH CREATION OF THIS WORK WAS COMPLETED This information must be given in all cases.
◀ Year

DATE AND NATION OF FIRST PUBLICATION OF THIS PARTICULAR WORK
Complete this information ONLY if this work has been published.
Month ▶_____ Day ▶_____ Year ▶_____
◀ Nation

4

See instructions before completing this space

COPYRIGHT CLAIMANT(S) Name and address must be given even if the claimant is the same as the author given in space 2.▼

TRANSFER If the claimant(s) named here in space 4 are different from the author(s) named in space 2, give a brief statement of how the claimant(s) obtained ownership of the copyright.▼

APPLICATION RECEIVED

ONE DEPOSIT RECEIVED

TWO DEPOSITS RECEIVED

REMITTANCE NUMBER AND DATE

DO NOT WRITE HERE
OFFICE USE ONLY

MORE ON BACK ▶   • Complete all applicable spaces (numbers 5-11) on the reverse side of this page.
• See detailed instructions.   • Sign the form at line 10.

DO NOT WRITE HERE

Page 1 of____pages

EXAMINED BY	**FORM TX**

CHECKED BY

☐ CORRESPONDENCE
  Yes

☐ DEPOSIT ACCOUNT
  FUNDS USED

FOR
COPYRIGHT
OFFICE
USE
ONLY

DO NOT WRITE ABOVE THIS LINE. IF YOU NEED MORE SPACE, USE A SEPARATE CONTINUATION SHEET.

PREVIOUS REGISTRATION Has registration for this work, or for an earlier version of this work, already been made in the Copyright Office?

☐ **Yes** ☐ **No** If your answer is "Yes," why is another registration being sought? (Check appropriate box) ▼

☐ This is the first published edition of a work previously registered in unpublished form.

☐ This is the first application submitted by this author as copyright claimant.

☐ This is a changed version of the work, as shown by space 6 on this application.

If your answer is "Yes," give: **Previous Registration Number** ▼   **Year of Registration** ▼

5

DERIVATIVE WORK OR COMPILATION Complete both space 6a & 6b for a derivative work; complete only 6b for a compilation.

a. Preexisting Material Identify any preexisting work or works that this work is based on or incorporates. ▼

b. Material Added to This Work Give a brief, general statement of the material that has been added to this work and in which copyright is claimed. ▼

6

See instructions
before completing
this space.

7

—space deleted—

REPRODUCTION FOR USE OF BLIND OR PHYSICALLY HANDICAPPED INDIVIDUALS   A signature on this form at space 10, and a check in one of the boxes here in space 8, constitutes a non-exclusive grant of permission to the Library of Congress to reproduce and distribute solely for the blind and physically handicapped and under the conditions and limitations prescribed by the regulations of the Copyright Office: (1) copies of the work identified in space 1 of this application in Braille (or similar tactile symbols); or (2) phonorecords embodying a fixation of a reading of that work; or (3) both.

    a ☐ Copies and Phonorecords   **b** ☐ Copies Only   **c** ☐ Phonorecords Only

8

See instructions.

DEPOSIT ACCOUNT If the registration fee is to be charged to a Deposit Account established in the Copyright Office, give name and number of Account.

Name ▼   **Account Number** ▼

CORRESPONDENCE Give name and address to which correspondence about this application should be sent. Name/Address/Apt/City/State/Zip ▼

Area Code & Telephone Number ▶

9

Be sure to
give your
daytime phone
◀ number

CERTIFICATION*   I, the undersigned, hereby certify that I am the

Check one ▶

☐ author
☐ other copyright claimant
☐ owner of exclusive right(s)
☐ authorized agent of _____

of the work identified in this application and that the statements made by me in this application are correct to the best of my knowledge.

Name of author or other copyright claimant, or owner of exclusive right(s) ▲

Typed or printed name and date ▼ If this is a published work, this date must be the same as or later than the date of publication given in space 3.

_____ date ▶ _____

☞ Handwritten signature (X) ▼

10

MAIL CERTIFICATE TO

Name ▼

Number/Street/Apartment Number ▼

City/State/ZIP ▼

Certificate will be mailed in window envelope

Have you:
• Completed all necessary spaces?
• Signed your application in space 10?
• Enclosed check or money order for $10 payable to *Register of Copyrights*?
• Enclosed your deposit material with the application and fee?

MAIL TO: Register of Copyrights, Library of Congress, Washington, D.C. 20559.

11

APPENDIX H

TRADEMARK/SERVICE MARK QUESTIONAIRE

1. MARK_____ *

2. Date of first use in connection with your product or service: _____

3. Date the mark was first used in Interstate Commerce (date for first sale of your product or service):

   _____

4. The mark is used in connection with:_____

   _____ **

5. How is the mark affixed to the goods or used in connection with the service:_____

   _____ ***

6. Who will be the owner of the mark (Choose only one)?

   Individual

   _____
   Name

   _____
   Address

   _____
   Citizenship

   Corporation

   _____
   Exact Name of the Corporation****

   _____
   Address

   _____
   State of Incorporation

   _____
   Name of President

* If the mark is used in connection with a design or in a distinctive script, please attach a copy of the mark showing the design features or stylized script.

** Please list all of the goods and/or services. Be specific. If the mark has not yet been used on the goods/services, list all of the anticipated goods and services.

*** For goods this is usually done on labels, silk screened, printed, etched, etc. For services this is usually on advertisements, brochures, newspaper advertisements, yellow pages, flyers and the like.

**** As the name appears in the Articles of Incorporation.

Partnership

_____
Name of Partnership

_____
Name of Partner*****

_____
Address

_____
Citizenship of Partner

_____
Name of Partner

_____
Address

_____
Citizenship of Partner

7. Please return five examples of the mark as it is actually used in connection with your product or service. If the mark is not currently being used, please let us know as soon as it is.

For a TRADEMARK use examples such as labels, tags, or photographs of the mark if it is engraved or stamped on the goods.

For a SERVICEMARK use examples of actual advertisements, brochures, or other documentation showing the services being offered.

8. If the mark contains a foreign work or phrase or a corruption or derivation of a foreign word or phrase, please not the English translation.

***** We must have the name, address, and citizenship of every partner.

APPENDIX I

STATE MULTIPLES LAW

California, Cal. Civ. Code §§ 1740–45 (West Supp. 1992)

Georgia, Ga. Code Ann. §§ 10–1–431 to 10–1–433 (1986)

Hawaii, Haw. Rev. Stat. § 481F (Supp. 1991)

Illinois, Ill. Ann. Stat. ch. 121½ ¶¶ 361 *et seq.* (Smith–Hurd Supp. 1991)

Maryland, Md. Com. Law Code 14–501 to 14–505 (1991)

Michigan, Mich. Comp. Laws §§ 442.351–.367 (1991)

Minnesota, Minn. Stat. §§ 324.08–.10 (1992)

New York, N.Y. Arts & Cult. Aff. Law §§ 15.01–.19 (McKinney Supp. 1992)

North Carolina, N.C. Gen. Stat. §§ 25C–10 to 25C–16 (Michie 1989)

Oregon, Or. Rev. Stat. §§ 359.300–.315 (1991)

South Carolina, S.C. Code Ann. §§ 39–16–10 to 39–16–50 (Supp. 1990)

APPENDIX J

CERTIFICATE OF AUTHENTICITY, OWNERSHIP AND VALUE— INERNATIONAL ART REGISTRY LIMITED
(Modified by Author)

CERTIFICATE OF AUTHENTICITY, OWNERSHIP AND VALUE

THIS IS TO CERTIFY that The International Art Registry Limited (hereinafter referred to as the Registry) is chartered by the State of New York to issue certificates and valuations in respect of works of fine art; and that the Registry has independently examined the work of fine art evidenced by Certificate Number ___ and Registration Number ___ expiring on _____, and that the work of fine art is of the authorship, ownership and value indicated in the space provided herein; and that for liability damages arising out of errors or omissions the work of fine art is valued at $_____.

ARTIST
TITLE
MEDIUM
PAPER SIZE   IMAGE SIZE
PAPER   EDGE
DATE   SIGNATURE
EDITION & NUMBER   ARTIST'S PROOFS   OTHER PROOFS
TOTAL UNITS REGISTERED   NUMBER OF IMPRESSIONS OR CASTINGS
PROOF OF CANCELLATION OR DESTRUCTION OF MOLD
LOCATION OF CHOPS
PRINTER
PUBLISHER
REMARKS
The rightful owner of the above described work of fine art is
    Name
    Address
    City   State   Zip

In our judgment the current fair market value (*what a willing buyer will pay a willing seller on the open market*) of the above described work of art is $_____.

This certification terminates upon the transfer of the work of fine art or upon the expiration of the Certificate of Registration.

THE INTERNATIONAL ART REGISTRY LIMITED
PRESIDENT _____

   NOTICE: Be advised to contact the Home Office of The International Art Registry Limited in order to confirm that this Certificate is in full force and effect.

INSURANCE

The Registry maintains insurance coverage to pay on its behalf all sums which it shall become legally obligated to pay as damages arising out of any negligent act, errors or omissions, committed or alleged to have been committed by the Registry while in the performance of professional services of verifying the Authenticity, Ownership and Value of works of art of all kinds. Written evidence (a Certificate of Insurance) of this insurance coverage is available upon request from the Home Office of the Registry.

©The International Art Registry Limited 1976

APPENDIX K

STATE MORAL RIGHTS ACTS

California Art Preservation Act, Ann. Cal. Civ. Code § 987

Connecticut Art Preservation & Artists' Rights Statute, § 42–116s

Louisiana Artists' Authorship Rights Act, 1986 La. Acts 599, ch. 32

Maine Moral Rights Statute, Me. Rev. Stat. Ann. tit. 27, § 303

Massachusetts Moral Rights Statute, Mass. Ann. Laws ch. 231, § 85s, ch. 260 § 2c

Nevada Miscellaneous Trade Regulations—Works of Art, N.R.S. §§ 598.970–.978

New Mexico Act Relating to Fine Art in Public Buildings, N.M. Stat. Ann. § 13–4b–2

New York Artists' Authorship Rights Act, art. 12j, N.Y. Gen. Bus. Law §§ 228 *et seq.*

Pennsylvania Fine Arts Preservation Act, 1986 Pa. Laws no. 161, Pa. Stat. Ann. tit. 73, §§ 2101, 2121

Rhode Island Artists' Rights Act, 1987 R.I. Pub. Laws 566

Utah Percent-for-Art Statute, Moral Rights Provision, Utah Code Ann. § 64–2a–9

Index